UNASHAMED
OF
THE **GOSPEL**

UNASHAMED
OF
THE **GOSPEL**

The Conference Messages of
T4G 2014

JONATHAN **LEEMAN**
General Editor

PUBLISHING GROUP
Nashville, Tennessee

978-1-4336-8897-3

Printed by B&H Publishing Group
Nashville, Tennessee

Dewey Decimal Classification: 248.5
Subject Heading: WITNESSING \ CHRISTIAN LIFE \
GOSPEL

1 2 3 4 5 6 7 8 • 20 19 18 17 16

CONTENTS

FOREWORD

Suppose you were suddenly to find yourself among seven thousand mainly young people. Suppose they were singing, without any band, Reginald Heber's "Holy, holy, holy, Lord God Almighty!" Suppose after that singing you heard an hour-long sermon, and that all this went on for three days. You might well wonder where you were and why this was happening.

My own arrival in that situation was not entirely sudden, for I had heard and read of it beforehand. But it has still left me with a degree of wonder. The place was the Together for the Gospel conference in Louisville, Kentucky, in April of 2014. Until then, I had not been in a city before where I was stopped in the street, and at its airport, to sign Banner of Truth books.

What is happening in the United States? Too often an opinion is offered by those dependent on secondhand information. It is further regrettable that, due to one publisher's subtitle nearly a decade ago, "A Journalist's Journey with the New Calvinism," the idea was launched that what is happening can be called "the New Calvinist movement." That umbrella label is a misnomer. A "movement" suggests organization, staff, office, and, usually, its own magazine and conference. The phenomenon being described has none of these things. It is far more indefinite and diverse.

There is another reason why the name coined in 2008 should not be accepted: "New Calvinist" too easily suggests some kind

of departure from "the Old." But what is now occurring in many
parts of the United States can clearly be seen to have sprung out
of what is far from new. It is no more "new" than the doctrine
that was heard under Whitefield and Edwards in the 1740s—or,
later, under Spurgeon and Lloyd-Jones. What was supposed to be
"as dead as Queen Anne" is very much alive in what is happening today. Old authors are being read more eagerly than young
ones, and yet it is not the literature, significant as it is, which can
account for what is happening. The truth is,

> Nobody on earth has managed this Reformed resurgence
> with all its diversity. No one on earth has planned it, and
> none can or should harness it. This is a work of God. It
> may be short-lived, or it may be deep and wide and long.
> God will decide. I make no triumphalist predictions. We
> don't control it.[1]

Archibald Brown once told the declining congregation at the
Metropolitan Tabernacle that, when God revives his work, popular
solutions for a recovery would disappear: "There will be nothing
said from the pulpit or platform about 'up-to-date.' . . . It will be
Bible! Bible! Bible! And the people clamoring, 'Let us have the
Word of God!'"[2] The phenomenon I am discussing does not profess
to be a revival, but it is appealing to the Bible in a new way, challenging the perceived wisdom of much contemporary evangelicalism. Not without reason, Jonathan Leeman writes: "The hope of
T4G and other like-minded conferences and organizations in the
present day is that they would represent not the culmination of
revival, but the kindling."[3]

Of course, anything seen to be influential in the church scene
gathers supporters, and it is to be expected that all kinds of group-
ings, churches, and conferences may wish to align themselves with
a resurgent Calvinism. A mixture of participants is inevitable. It

has always been so. As Edwards pointed out in the revival of religion in the 1740s, some of its most ardent enthusiasts proved to be no true helpers in the work of God.[4] The adoption of a name is no proof of anything. Everything needs to be tested by the truth proclaimed, and the character of those involved—are they prayerful, humble before God, and loving to all men?

The United States is a large nation, and it would be folly to make generalizations about this resurgence. As I have already said, there is no one bloc organization to which either credit or blame can be given. The T4G conference is only one conference out of many similar ones across the States, yet to a considerable extent it may be thought of as representative of what some have dubbed "New Calvinism." Of the nine men who preached—including Thabiti Anyabwile, Mark Dever, Ligon Duncan, John MacArthur, Albert Mohler, and John Piper—none used that name, but they have been so identified by others.

This Louisville conference originated in 2006, and has met biennially since. What it stands for is unambiguous. It has eighteen Articles of Faith printed in the conference program, and the addresses given at the earlier conferences are available online.[5] They will make surprising reading for anyone who supposes that this is just another of the recurring cycles of evangelical enterprises intent on drawing a crowd. Instead of following a well-trodden evangelical pragmatism, T4G departs from much that has been near axiomatic in contemporary thinking. I had scarcely returned home to the United Kingdom when I ran into that thinking in an article which told me that the kind of worship service and preaching that was part of the ministry of Dr. Lloyd-Jones belonged to an age "completely gone."

Such bold assertions received no reverence at T4G. Instead, the concern over what "appeals" to people, or "turns them off," is traced to a lost confidence in the power of the gospel itself.

The role which Christian music is expected to play in influencing the world for the gospel is a prominent issue today. Here, also, T4G is out of step with popular thinking. I do not say that it has entirely clarified the issue, but it is addressing and emphasizing the right starting point. Namely, worship ought to be worship.

In Louisville, the words sung for praise were selected chiefly for the suitability of their biblical content. Some two-thirds of the hymns printed in the conference brochure were composed before 1900, and a number much earlier. But it was not only what was sung, but how it was sung, which stood out. Today congregational singing is commonly fast, and frequently almost drowned out by accompanying musical instruments. What else can possibly be popular? Slow singing, led only by a piano (and sometimes not even by that), is supposed to be something to be avoided. Certainly there is no merit in slow singing as such, and there has to be variation in pace, but when the tempo is always quick the strong likelihood is that the music has come to mean more than the words. Spurgeon represented what he called "the new fashioned style of singing" as, "Let us rattle through it as fast as we can. Never mind about whether God gets any glory out of it or not; all we care about is the music." He recommended tunes that give you "a chance of chewing it, not one that you must swallow, as if it were a pill."

There were other areas where the teaching or practice at Together for the Gospel cannot be said to harmonize well with contemporary thinking. No ground was given to the cry that "we are in the visual age," not in the age of the spoken word; nor to the idea that the so-called "generational divide" should be reflected in the organization of church life. Young although the majority of the conference was, the leadership was not.

The leadership of T4G has varied little from its beginning in 2006, and the unity of the conference program reflects the unity among its planners. Although they are preachers from different denominational backgrounds, there is a strong friendship among them. One of the factors that has brought them together is the heritage of literature to which they have a common commitment. This literature was present at Louisville, and urged upon the attendees, in an unforgettable manner. Both the quantity and the consistent character of the books available in rooms the size of football fields were quite staggering. No reformed publisher seemed to be missing. In the course of the proceedings, when books were given to particular participants, the choice of titles was significant. The youngest pastor present was given Arnold Dallimore's two-volume life of Whitefield; the longest-serving preacher was given *Archibald G. Brown: Spurgeon's Successor*; someone else received the 1,200 pages of William Gurnall's classic, *The Christian in Complete Armour*. By no means were all the authors commended deceased. Thabiti Anyabwile spoke of how reading Walter J. Chantry's book, *Today's Gospel: Authentic or Synthetic?* had been a turning point in his thinking and that he had "lived in the wake of it ever since."

At the same time, it was clear that such books were being recommended because they served the primary purpose of the conference, which is to see the gospel itself advanced. The gospel was uppermost, and it was also served by the short film recordings in which a whole variety of individuals spoke of how they came to know Christ. These were valuable and moving to hear.

Together for the Gospel is not a "church" movement; the focus is to help local churches and pastors. In the words of Article XIV of the conference:

> We affirm that the shape of Christian discipleship is
> congregational, that God's purpose is evident in faithful
> Gospel congregations. . . . We deny that any Christian

can truly be a faithful disciple apart from the teaching, discipline, fellowship, and accountability of a congregation of fellow disciples, organized as a Gospel church. We further deny that the Lord's Supper can faithfully be administered apart from the right practice of church discipline.

The elimination of all differences is no part of the T4G program, and disagreements over some points of the Bible, such as those which separate churches, were not treated as a threat to unity in the gospel.

Martyn Lloyd-Jones, a name often mentioned at the conference, once replied to a questioner who asked if he thought revival was near. The doctor said he did not, "because we are too healthy." No such supposed "healthiness" was encouraged in the addresses at Louisville. The call for greater prayerfulness and compassion for those out of Christ was strong. There were plain warnings against "carnal enthusiasm," and MacArthur, preaching from John 6 about the crowd which deserted Christ, warned against putting any trust in numbers. If any had come only to hear a favorite preacher they would have been disappointed, for the time when various men were to speak was not announced beforehand. We were urged instead to look to the Word of God. As John Piper has written:

Disillusion often follows naive admiration. . . . There is none without sin, and all our triumphs are mixed with imperfection. . . . All this I say to caution us from transferring the root of our exaltation from the historic Word of God written to the contemporary work of God reported. God alone never changes, but the outpourings of his blessings ebb and flow in ways far too mysterious for our small minds to judge.[6]

Yet the concluding note must be of thanksgiving. There is a wonderful reviving power in the Word of God! Prayer is being heard and a new generation is rising! "Let thy work appear unto thy servants, and thy glory unto their children."

—Iain Murray[7]

INTRODUCTION

They were plain words: "Things look bad right now." Yet it was this unadorned, blunt assessment—spoken by Mark Dever as the first sentence of the first talk—that captured a feeling that hung in the room throughout the three-day pastors' conference of April 2014.

Only two years had elapsed since the 2012 Together for the Gospel event. But for those of us who attended both, the two years felt as if they might have been two generations as measured by the rate of cultural change. Such was the direction of court rulings, news events, and other indicators of rapidly shifting moral standards in the United States in the twenty-four intervening months. Something all around us felt heavier, darker, like sensing a barometric shift that signals a coming storm.

The topic of the conference therefore felt intimidating, profound, appropriate: evangelism, or "the unashamed gospel." In his talk, Matt Chandler captured the connection precisely:

> My great fear for Christians in America is that, in an area where we already perceive ourselves to be weak, all the talk about how acidic the air has become might cause us to shrink back even more, instead of letting the Bible encourage us to enter more boldly into what God will do to save the lost.

Again and again, the conference talks, now the chapters of this book, traded back and forth between these two realities: yes, the culture has become more hostile, but God's Word can be trusted; yes, our gospel message appears exclusive, but that exclusive Word is the only hope of the nations; yes, our sin and the sin of our non-Christian friends is great, but Jesus can actually make us clean!

The talks have been reordered in this volume for the purpose of giving the table of contents a narrative arch, as in, "Here are some of the particular challenges; here are some of the reasons our churches can be unashamed in the face of those challenges; and here now is how we must move forward."

Matt Chandler's meditation on 2 Timothy 1:8–14, "Unashamed When the Weather Worsens," comes first because it sums up the whole arch. After its triumphant beginning, the weather had worsened in the city of Ephesus, where Timothy pastored. So Paul offers him several reasons why he could unashamedly press ahead, even into suffering, as Paul had done: God saves; nothing ever depended on our strength to begin with; death is dead; and our God is big. So hold fast to these promises, brother pastor!

R. Albert Mohler focuses on the challenge of the exclusivity of the message of Jesus Christ. That message presents itself as the *only right way*, and such exclusivity is becoming more culturally obnoxious by the hour. Christians might be tempted to shy away from this message, but, as Mohler puts it, "If we see it as a negative, hard, burdensome truth that we are forced by Christian duty to bear, we slander the gospel. We are those who must strive to celebrate the gospel in every dimension, even its exclusivity. The singularity of Christ is what saves us."

John MacArthur begins with an autobiographical account of why he has always had a ministry of trying to reach the reached— or evangelizing the church. Few things grieve him as a pastor more than watching someone who turns out to be a counterfeit

Christian walk away from the faith. And what do we make of such defectors? Should they discourage evangelism? Not at all! MacArthur then walks through John 6 in order to identify a few characteristics of false believers, to contrast those with the characteristics of true believers, and then to offer a word of comfort and peace to believers when they watch the defections.

The next four chapters, like four pillars, provide support for Christian and pastoral confidence for sharing the gospel unashamedly. Thabiti Anyabwile looks closely at the text of the Prodigal Son, glances up the page at the two parables before it, and notices what they all have in common: all three focus on what causes heaven to rejoice—the repentance of sinners. Why then would we ever shrink back from calling sinners to repentance? It causes heaven to rejoice, and what must that sound like!

Mark Dever walks slowly and sweetly through the jaw-dropping, confidence-giving, suspenseful but not surprising story around which the book of Isaiah centers the account of King Hezekiah's response to the encroaching and undefeatable Assyrian army in Isaiah 36 and 37. The lesson is a crucial one for Christians when the cultural weather worsens: if God is with us, we cannot fail.

Kevin DeYoung starts with the observation that we will only be as confident in our evangelism as we are confident in the truth of God's Word. So are God's Word and God's promises true? Can we trust them? Some belonging to the church contest the inerrancy of God's Word. When they do, however, they depart from Jesus. They aren't just giving away a doctrine devised by nineteenth-century Presbyterians, says DeYoung, they are giving away Jesus. A Christian, when he evangelizes, can put all the trust in Scripture that Jesus himself put into it—total trust.

J. Ligon Duncan, as in 2012, draws percipiently from the Old Testament in order to preach the glories of the gospel of Christ.

Read through Leviticus, and it's easy to wonder what all these strange cleanliness laws have to do with Christianity. Suppose a man's wife contracts a skin disease, or she touches a dead body. The law says she must go outside the camp for a time because she's unclean. What? Is that fair? Well, hold on, says Duncan. Maybe God has something for us even here. Could it be that these laws point toward the power and perfect righteousness of God's Son? Just think, what happened when the Son touched the diseased or dead person? Read Duncan's answer. If the global West is enduring a time of moral decline, here is the Savior we all so desperately need.

Pastors and Christians can be unashamed in the sharing and proclaiming of the gospel because heaven rejoices in the repentance of sinners, because God's victory is certain, because his promises are unbreakable, and because Jesus is precisely the Savior that this broken and unclean world needs.

The final two chapters provide us with the "what now?". The answer, in two words, is *plead* and *pray*, which brings us finally to John Piper and David Platt.

Both Piper and Platt's chapters, on Romans 9 and Exodus 32—33 respectively, affirm the sovereignty of God in all things. And then both lean heavily toward our responsibility to plead with unbelievers and to pray desperately for them. Piper specifically examines how the doctrine of divine election should impact our practice of evangelism. The short answer is, it should humble us, it should impel us to persuade, and it should push us to pray.

Yet Platt spends nearly his entire talk on this last point: how we should plead with God in prayer. He begins with this observation:

> It's dangerously possible for you and me to carry on the
> machinery and activity of the churches we lead, and all
> of it can be smooth, even successful; and we may never

notice that the Spirit is totally absent from it. If we're not careful, we can deceive ourselves, mistaking the presence of physical bodies in a building for the existence of spiritual life in a church. I wonder if the greatest hindrance to the advancement of the gospel in our day may be the attempt of the people of God to do the work of God apart from the power of the Spirit of God. The greatest barrier to the spread of the gospel may not be the self-indulgent immorality of our culture, but our self-sufficient mentality in the church, which is evident in our prayerlessness.

How easy it is not to pray! How easily self-sufficiency creeps in! But is this not foolish?

Mark Dever has written elsewhere that, when we evangelize, "we are evangelizing the cemetery." We are asking God to take people who are spiritually dead and to give them life. There has never been a time or place or culture in which it was natural for people to repent. The work of the church and the pastor is supernatural work. Only God can do it. "From that standpoint," Dever concludes, "recent cultural changes have made our job zero percent harder."[8]

If anyone should recognize the folly of self-sufficiency, it should be people evangelizing the cemetery. Desperate prayer is the only rational response.

Our postures toward God should be that of the man in Jesus' parable who knocks on his friend's door at night asking for three loaves of bread. The friend may be inclined to say through the door that it's locked and that his children are in bed. Yet customs in the ancient Near East being what they were, Jesus observes, "I tell you, even though he will not get up and give you the bread because of friendship, yet because of your shameless audacity he will surely get up and give you as much as you need" (Luke 11:8 NIV).

We, too, should approach God with shameless audacity. We must audaciously ask for opportunities to proclaim the gospel, and audaciously ask for the opportunity to see conversions. Never do we depart from the attitude of "Thy will be done." But Jesus instructs us to ask audaciously nonetheless. He goes on to summarize the lesson of the parable like this:

> "So I say to you, keep asking, and it will be given to you. Keep searching, and you will find. Keep knocking, and the door will be opened to you. For everyone who asks receives, and the one who searches finds, and to the one who knocks, the door will be opened. What father among you, if his son asks for a fish, will give him a snake instead of a fish? Or if he asks for an egg, will give him a scorpion? If you then, who are evil, know how to give good gifts to your children, how much more will the heavenly Father give the Holy Spirit to those who ask him?" (Luke 11:9–13 HCSB)

Such asking and knocking is the only reasonable course of action when evangelizing a cemetery.

Tragically, we are not reasonable. We do not ask. And God, as a quiet act of judgment, sometimes grants our self-sufficient hearts what they seek, even in ministry. Can you not think of some "godly" pursuit in which you were utterly prayerless and faithless, and yet you attained your goal anyway? Such successes only affirm us in our self-sufficiency.

But things do indeed look bad right now, as Dever observed. And hopefully, staring into the demonic face of all the bad, the strong man of hell and death who is mightier than we, will force us to the end of our self-sufficiency. Hopefully, each of us and our churches will resolve, "Lord, we are tired of trying to see what we can do. We want to see what *you* can do."

Indeed, the hope of every pastor author in this volume is that every pastor-reader would lose interest in seeing what he can personally build, but would instead ask the Lord to show, to demonstrate, to prove what the Lord alone can build—and to ask audaciously.

Don't you want that, Christian? Haven't you got a pretty good idea already of what *you* can accomplish in your evangelism? Don't you want to see what *God* can accomplish? Ask him.

I pray this book will help you to know that you can.

—Jonathan Leeman

CHAPTER 1

Unashamed When the Weather Worsens
(2 Timothy 1:8–14)

Matt Chandler

The idea of being unashamed in evangelism, for me, is an extremely personal thing. I remember walking off my high school football field into the locker room. A wide receiver on our team walked up to me and said, "Hey, I need to tell you about Jesus. When do you want to do that?"

To this day, I like that approach. He didn't say, "Would you like to hear about Jesus?" He basically said, "I'm gonna let you decide when this conversation about Jesus occurs, but this conversation is going to happen."

Through the unashamed boldness of this passionate, Bible-believing man of God, God brought me forth.

The Christianity I had seen before that point was hardly compelling. My father was not interested in Christ at all. In fact, he was a terrible, abusive man before Jesus saved him. And my mom thought the Pharisees were a bit too loose in how they applied the law. So I wanted nothing to do with my mother's Jesus, but I also didn't want the licentiousness represented by my abusive, bitter, dried-up father. Jeff Faircloth, the man who approached me in the football locker room, was the first person I saw who really loved the gospel.

Jeff began taking me to his Baptist church and their Wednesday night youth gathering entitled JAM, which stood for "Jesus And Me." I learned very quickly that Christians liked acronyms in a way that the rest of the world doesn't. I also discovered the most kitschy, ridiculous thing in the history of the Christian church. We would sing songs about having joy down in our hearts—deep, deep down in our hearts. And then: "Now spell it!" To my horror as an unbelieving, unchurched young man, they would spell the word *joy* with their bodies while singing. The entire thing reeked of a bad *Saturday Night Live* sketch.

Jeff would then drive me home, and I would mock what I just heard and saw the whole way. He would lovingly and patiently endure the mocking. It's funny now to look back on those days with theological lenses. I didn't have a category for the effectual call of God. So I would mock the entire way home: "This is so ridiculous. How can you even believe that?" Jeff would drop me off at my house and ask if I wanted to come back, to which I'd respond, "Yeah. Can you pick me up? I don't have a ride."

I now know what God was doing. He was wooing. He was drawing. I had no clue: "You want me to go this way, God? Okay."

About a year later, the Lord opened my heart to belief and wrecked me. I actually remember thinking, "Oh no, he got me." And from there I loved him so much that I lost my mind for a bit— in a good way. I bought a T-shirt that said "I ♥ Jesus" and wore it all the time. I would tell anyone who would listen about Jesus. My evangelistic tactics were terrible, yet as goofy as they were, God drew people with them.

The first guy I tried to share my faith with was a friend with whom I had been running around doing terrible things, Jimmy Hereford. Jimmy saw what was happening to me and started asking, "What in the world! I 'heart' Jesus?! What did they do to you, bro?"

I didn't know much theology at this point. I knew there was hell, and you didn't want to go there. I knew you needed to love Jesus. And I knew he died on the cross to forgive sin—and that his forgiveness somehow worked in between hell and love. So I would lean on Jimmy with the threat of hell. My first shot at explaining the gospel of Jesus Christ to Jimmy focused on how Jesus saves us from hell and what hell was.

Almost all of our discussions revolved around fire and hell. A couple of weeks later, I was sitting in the stands watching a junior varsity game. Jimmy was next to me when another guy walked into the gym whom Jimmy hated. He said he wanted to fight the guy. I told him to be careful because the guy might kill him. Jimmy replied, "I ain't afraid to die."

I went right back to the issue of hell: "Jimmy, do you remember that hell thing we talked about? You better get that cleaned up first."

About a week later I was eating a piece of candy. Jimmy asked me if I had any more. I pulled them out of my pocket, and said, "Yeah, but the only ones I have are fire." He replied that he didn't care for fire. So I said, "Remember when we talked? If you don't like fire, you need to consider the things that I've been telling you about Jesus."

Then Jimmy came to JAM with me. I started thinking, *Oh man, I'm that guy now. I'm bringing someone to JAM. I know what I'm going to hear on the car ride home.*

That night at JAM there was no preaching. Instead, we watched a terrible video called *Hell's Bells* about secular music. The video said that if you listened to secular music, you'd end up doing methamphetamines and maybe kill one of your parents. Of course the movie was dated with bands we weren't listening to, like Journey. I don't think Jimmy even knew who Journey was.

Halfway through the movie, Jimmy leaned over to me and said, "Hey man, I want to do it." I was like, "Bro, you can't kill your parents. If you kill your folks, you're going to jail."

Somehow from there, Jimmy trusted in Christ. He believed from *Hell's Bells*. It was an evangelistic train wreck, and he believed.

Jimmy is thirty-something now with a wife and children. He's a man of God helping a church plant in Dallas get off the ground and he's the best evangelist I've been around.

In fact, I'll put an exclamation point on God's faithfulness in this story. Jimmy got a job at a Mexican food restaurant and began to share the gospel with some of the waiters there, including one man by the name of Carl Brower. After six months of hearing the good news of the gospel from Jimmy, Carl gave his life to Jesus Christ. Carl fell in love with Jesus, and we happened to hire Carl Brower several years ago at The Village Church to run our pre-school ministry. In the Lord's sweet mercy on my life, Carl Brower has held two of my children and prayed that Christ would save their souls.

So when we talk about being unashamed in evangelism, I can feel it. I feel it because somebody came and got me. God sent someone to boldly walk up to me and say, "I need to tell you about Jesus. When do you want to do this?"

Most of us already feel a bit guilty about evangelism because we know we're not doing it like we should. And now, how many news reports and sermons keep telling us that our culture is getting darker? That the environment is growing more hostile? That it's getting harder to be a Christian?

My great fear for Christians in America is that, in an area where we already perceive ourselves to be weak, all the talk about how acidic the air has become might cause us to shrink back even more, instead of letting the Bible encourage us to enter more boldly into what God will do to save the lost. What we are experiencing is not new under the sun. Yes, there might be growing hostility toward believers in Christ. No, we should not respond as if we are the first generation that will have to weather this. That simply is not true.

A Turn for the Worse in the Ephesian Weather

The birth of the church in Ephesus is one of the most spectacular things to witness in the Bible. Paul shows up right after Apollos, who was a good preacher, but had to be corrected. Then Paul rolls in, finds some disciples, and begins to preach. He moves from the synagogue into the Hall of Tyrannus and reasons with the people for a couple of years. There, the Bible tells us, all the residents of Asia heard the Word of the Lord, both Jews and Greeks (Acts 19:10).

The gospel then begins to take root in Ephesus in a profound way. A number of Jewish exorcists get beat up by a demon-possessed man. Fear falls on everyone, and the name of Jesus is extolled (Acts 19:17). Then we read,

> Also many of those who were now believers came, confessing and divulging their practices. And a number of those who had practiced magic arts brought their books together and burned them in the sight of all. And they counted the value of them and found it came to fifty

thousand pieces of silver. So the word of the Lord continued to increase and prevail mightily. (vv. 18–19)

How mightily did the Word of God prevail in Ephesus? So
mightily that a group of men who made money selling idols could
no longer sell them because of gospel belief, and they started a
riot.

Can you get your head around the idea of the gospel making
such headway in a city that no more dollars can be made from sinful gain? On the freeways of Dallas I constantly pass strip clubs. I
wonder what it would be like if no one spent money at Dallas strip
clubs because the gospel had permeated our culture so thoroughly,
forcing the owners to riot. When I see those clubs, I pray, "Let the
money dry up. Let the money dry up because of gospel belief."

That's what happens in Ephesus in Acts 19. That's how the
church begins.

But then Paul promises a change in the weather will come. In
chapter 20, Paul warns the Ephesian elders, "I know that after my
departure fierce wolves will come in among you, not sparing the
flock" (v. 29). And by the time we get to 2 Timothy, Paul says, "all
who are in Asia turned away from me" (1:15). That's a change in
the weather, for sure.

We started with, "All in Asia heard the word of the Lord and
the idol-makers were pitching a fit." And we arrived at, "I'm in
chains in Rome, and everyone has deserted me." The temperature
has dropped.

And yet.

It is in this environment that Paul writes to Timothy concerning what to do when the weather worsens.

Therefore do not be ashamed of the testimony about
our Lord, nor of me his prisoner, but share in suffering
for the gospel by the power of God, who saved us and

called us to a holy calling, not because of our works but because of his own purpose and grace, which he gave us in Christ Jesus before the ages began, and which now has been manifested through the appearing of our Savior Christ Jesus, who abolished death and brought life and immortality to light through the gospel, for which I was appointed a preacher and apostle and teacher, which is why I suffer as I do. But I am not ashamed, for I know whom I have believed, and I am convinced that he is able to guard until that Day what has been entrusted to me. Follow the pattern of the sound words that you have heard from me, in the faith and love that are in Christ Jesus. By the Holy Spirit who dwells within us, guard the good deposit entrusted to you. (2 Tim. 1:8–14)

Don't Be Ashamed, But Share in the Suffering

Verse 8 sets the context. Paul tells Timothy, "Do not be ashamed of the testimony about our Lord," but instead, "share in suffering for the gospel by the power of God."

That is not the type of encouragement most pastors are looking for when the air is growing acidic. "You once had a lot of support. Now your support is drying up. But I still want you to step into the suffering, Timothy. Don't step around it. Step into it, and know you're going to suffer. Don't be surprised by this. Share in suffering for the gospel by the power of God."

There is so much material in the New Testament like this. It almost confuses me when Christians are surprised by suffering. How can you read the Bible and then be surprised when suffering shows up in your life—regardless of the form?

James says to "count it all joy . . . when you meet trials of various kinds" (1:2). Do you mean cancer, James? Yes, that's a "various kind." Do you mean people lying to me? Yeah, that's in there too. And persecution? Of course.

Jesus himself says, "Then they will deliver you up to tribulation and put you to death, and you will be hated by all nations for my name's sake. And then many will fall away and betray one another and hate one another. And many false prophets will arise and lead many astray" (Matt. 24:9–11).

Pastor, if you knew that suffering was going to be on your job description, the only reason you would do it is because you are called. Don't talk to me about any of this Christian celebrity, Hollywood nonsense. Put "share in suffering" on the job description, and let's see who is left. Everybody loves Pauline theology. But few of us want Pauline pain.

So many guys want to stand on the stage. But do you want Moses' stage? He enjoyed forty years in the desert with grumbling, complaining people and then doesn't get to go into the Promised Land. He dies on the mountain!

Or how about Jeremiah's stage? God lets him go into exile with everyone else. Jeremiah wonders if God has seduced him. Deceived him. Tricked him.

The idea of suffering should not surprise us when we think about the words used in the New Testament: tribulation and death, hated by all nations, people falling away, people betraying and hating one another, and false prophets arising from within the church.

The same thing is present in the book of Acts, a constant cycle of persecution and praise. A group hears the gospel, responds, and praises God. Then another group persecutes, marginalizes, and tries to destroy the first group. Think of Peter's sermons at Pentecost or Solomon's portico. Neither is seeker-friendly. Yet thousands come to know Christ. Peter also heals a man, and he's arrested for it.

It's always been like this. We may be in a day and age where the air is getting more acidic. We will suffer. But there is nowhere to run. You will be hated in all nations for Jesus' Name's sake.

Sitting in prison, abandoned by former associates, Paul knows this. And he knows bad days are coming for Timothy if they have not begun already (2 Tim. 3:1). False teachers and corrupt men will rise up who will lead people astray. He promises Timothy, "all who desire to live a godly life in Christ Jesus will be persecuted, while evil people and impostors will go on from bad to worse, deceiving and being deceived" (3:12–13).

If you are a pastor, you know that few things are more devastating than to watch people fall away from the faith. Or to watch hate begin to fester in the hearts of people whom we thought were the children of God. And how exhausting false teachers are!

So Paul is looking into Timothy's spiritual soul, knowing how timid and reserved Timothy can be. Paul's message is, "Prepare to suffer. You're not going to get around it. Prepare to suffer." But then Paul helps Timothy know how to suffer by the power of God. He gives him four things that would enable Timothy—and us—to walk in unashamed, emboldened passion for the name and renown of Jesus Christ in evangelism, even in an acidic culture.

Remember that God Saved and Called Us

First, we should be unashamed in our evangelism because we know that God has saved and called us. Listen to verses 8 and 9 again in chapter 1: "Therefore do not be ashamed of the testimony about our Lord, nor of me his prisoner, but share in suffering for the gospel by the power of God, *who saved us and called us to a holy calling*" (emphasis added).

Paul never got over his conversion. How could he? He was kicking open doors, dragging men and women into the street, and taking them to prison.

Paul was not a seeker. On the road to Damascus, he was not reading Tim Keller's latest book. He was not considering presuppositional apologetics. In fact, he describes himself as an "insolent opponent" (1 Tim. 1:13). Do you know what an insolent opponent is? It is someone who doesn't care about the facts or what's true. If you're married, here's what that looks like: You're deep into an argument with your spouse and you realize you are wrong, but it's too late. You aren't retracting or pulling back. You're in too deep. This was Paul.

But now his word to Timothy is, remember who called and saved us. Let's not get over the miracle of rebirth. Let's not forget that we were in the domain of darkness before God transferred us into the kingdom of his beloved Son. He saved us!

I have often wondered why I cared when Jeff shared the gospel with me and took me to JAM. Why did I keep going? I had all the reason in the world to doubt the goodness of God: an alcoholic and abusive father, a hyper-religious mother. I had a thousand reasons to think Christianity was nonsense. Yet the Lord kept wooing. Kept calling. Relentlessly pursuing. Now, therefore, I can be unashamed, knowing that what God did with me he will do with others.

You need to remember the same thing. *You* were saved and called.

Remember You Weren't Awesome to Begin With

Second, Paul reminds us in verse 9 that we were not awesome to begin with. We should not be ashamed but should share in suffering by the power of God, "who saved us and called us to a holy calling, *not because of our works but because of his own purpose and grace"* (emphasis added).

You and I were not saved because of our brilliance and savvy and good works. If God could only accomplish his purposes through the best and brightest, he would not be God. And the glory would not belong to him.

The more you think evangelism is about you, the less you will evangelize. You will always feel inadequate. You will never feel sharp enough. You will always get in the way of God saving and rescuing when you make it about you and your ability.

So I plead with you: Get over yourself. God is awesome. He doesn't need you to be awesome. He needs you to be obedient.

Good apologetics may remove hurdles. They are helpful. But I have never checkmated a brother in an argument and then had him start weeping, "I'm a sinner. I need a Savior!" God does that. The Spirit of God opens up hearts to belief. Our job is to tell and tell and tell and tell.

You were not saved because you are awesome. You were saved because God is. If you don't understand this, you will never be bold in evangelism. You will treat rejection as a rejection of you, which you cannot stand, when it's really a rejection of God. Clearly, there is still too much of you in the exchange. You are like the guy who runs his mouth about how good he is on the basketball court until he gets on the court.

The only One who is amazing in salvation is God. He is unreal. He is unbelievable. He is able—not you. I know you might fantasize about being intellectually clever. But it's God who saves.

Remember that Death Is Dead

The third thing to remember in order to be unashamed in evangelism is that death is dead, which we find in 2 Timothy 1:10.

Don't be ashamed but share in suffering by the power of God because grace has been shown to us "through the appearing of our Savior Christ Jesus, *who abolished death and brought life and immortality to light through the gospel*" (emphasis added).

Do you want to be emboldened in an acidic environment? Remember this: Your persecutors can't really do anything to you. What are they going to do—laugh at you? Put you in prison? Paul says in Philippians 1:21 that living is Christ and dying is gain. The most free you will ever be is when you get your mind around the fact that dying is gain. What then can they take from you?

The apostle Paul must have been so frustrating for the enemies of Christianity. You couldn't shut him down. Put him in prison? He converts all your guards and sings hymns while you torture him. Try to kill him? He looks forward to that. Let him live? He just keeps preaching. He knew Christ had overcome death and the grave.

I once heard Ravi Zacharias ask what a person could say to Lazarus to frighten him.

A persecutor: "We will kill you."

Lazarus: "Been there."

If Christ has conquered death, what can our persecutors do to us?

Remember Who Guards You—A Big God

I love Paul's last argument for why we can be unashamed in ministry and suffering: "I was appointed a preacher and apostle and teacher, which is why I suffer as I do. But I am not ashamed, for I know whom I have believed, and I am convinced that he is able to guard until that Day what has been entrusted to me" (2 Tim. 1:11–12).

The bigger God gets, the smaller we get and the more confidence we will have in boldly doing what God commands us to do. But the bigger we are, the smaller God is and the less confidence we will have to walk in obedience.

The tendency to think too highly of myself manifests itself too often in evangelism. Why wouldn't I share the gospel with the guy sitting next to me on the plane? Why don't I want to go across the street to my neighbor's house? The answer is, I'm too full of myself. I don't want to enter into this conversation because I think I might get rejected. There is still too much of me.

What do I do in response? I like to go to Job 38. I go here when I'm sick, feel inadequate, feel scared, or am full of myself.

> Then the LORD answered Job out of the whirlwind and said:
>
> "Who is this that darkens counsel by words without knowledge? Dress for action like a man; I will question you, you make it known to me. Where were you when I laid the foundation of the earth? Tell me, if you have understanding. Who determined its measurements— surely you know! Or who stretched the line upon it? On what were its bases sunk, or who laid its cornerstone, when the morning stars sang together and all the sons of God shouted for joy?
>
> "Or who shut in the sea with doors when it burst out from the womb, when I made clouds its garment and thick darkness its swaddling band, and prescribed limits for it and set bars and doors, and said, 'Thus far shall you come, and no farther, and here shall your proud waves be stayed'?
>
> "Have you commanded the morning since your days began, and caused the dawn to know its place, that it

might take hold of the skirt of the earth, and the wicked be shaken out of it? It is changed like clay under the seal, and its features stand out like a garment. From the wicked their light is withheld, and their uplifted arm is broken.

"Have you entered the springs of the sea, or walked in the recesses of the deep? Have the gates of death been revealed to you, or have you seen the gates of deep darkness? Have you comprehended the expanse of the earth? Declare, if you know all of this.

"Where is the way to the dwelling of the light, and where is the place of darkness, that you may take it to its territory and that you may discern the paths to its home? You know, for you were born then, and the number of your days is great!

"Have you entered the storehouses of the snow, or have you seen the storehouses of hail, which I have reserved for the time of trouble, for the day of battle and war? What is the way to the place where the light is distributed, or where the east wind is scattered upon the earth?

"Who has cleft a channel for the torrents of rain and a way for the thunderbolt, to bring rain on a land where man is, on the desert in which there is no man, to satisfy the waste of desolate land, and to make the ground sprout with grass?

"Has the rain a father, or who has begotten the drops of dew? From whose womb did the ice come forth, and who has given birth to the frost of heaven? The waters become hard like stone, and the face of the deep is frozen.

"Can you bind the chains of the Pleiades or loose the cords of Orion? Can you lead forth the Mazzaroth in their season, or can you guide the Bear with its children?

Do you know the ordinances of the heavens? And can you establish their rule on the earth?

"Can you lift up your voice to the clouds, that a flood of waters may cover you? Can you send forth lightnings, that they may go and say to you, 'Here we are'? Who has put wisdom in the inward parts or given understanding to the mind? Who can number the clouds by wisdom? Or who can tilt the waterskins of heavens, when the dust runs into a mass and the clods stick fast together?

"Can you hunt the prey for the lion, or satisfy the appetite of young lions, when they crouch in their dens or lie in wait in the thicket? Who provides for the raven its prey, when its young ones cry to God for help, and wander about for food?"

We could keep reading. The subsequent chapters continue to declare the bigness of God.

I go here because it reminds me that I cannot do anything. I have no good ideas. The passage is a warm blanket to my soul. It shakes me out of myself and reminds me that God saves. God draws. It's not my expertise. It's not my abilities or inabilities that matter. God and God alone saves. I need to remember him whom I have believed in, lest I start believing in me.

Our temptation is to narrow evangelism and conversion to a process. We even train our people in a system. Systems are appropriate and good at times. But no program or training system will ever produce a zeal for evangelism like knowing whom we have believed in.

Hold Fast to These Words

After providing Timothy with these four reasons for why he can be unashamed, Paul tells him to hold onto these instructions:

"Follow the pattern of the sound words that you have heard from me, in the faith and love that are in Christ Jesus. By the Holy Spirit who dwells within us, guard the good deposit entrusted to you" (2 Tim. 1:13–14).

Paul has just told Timothy not to sidestep suffering, but to enter into it. Those words make me think of the members of my church in Dallas. I have members who put their jobs on the line by sharing the gospel. Five years ago sharing the gospel meant they might not be invited to the Christmas party, but now they can lose their jobs. And what's Paul saying? Be willing to suffer and follow this pattern of sound words. Don't drift from what's true.

Paul knows there is going to be a strong pull away from sound words. We pastors will probably feel this more and more in the days ahead. We will feel it from our members. We will feel it from the ones who are zealous for evangelism. They will ask questions like, "Is that teaching really necessary? Do we really have to land on this side of that ethical issue? I mean, surely more people will get saved if we don't. Isn't that an open-handed issue where good Christians can disagree?"

In a place where the weather has changed, Paul responds to questions like these with, "You have to hold fast to sound doctrine!"

But he also tells us how to hold it: in faith and love. And holding it in faith and love brings us back to the big God. God is able and God has you. After all, in our present day, do we have any reason from history or Scripture to think that God will fail us? Or to think that God can be stopped?

Consider ancient Rome. It covered India to England for something like fifteen hundred years. They would have chuckled at America: "You guys have been around for what, a couple hundred years? You think you're something?" And there was a season when the Romans tried to destroy us Christians. They sawed us in two, boiled us alive, and threw us in front of lions. There was no Bill of Rights in Rome. Yet I read in one history book that by AD 351 some 50 percent of the Roman Empire called Jesus "Lord."

So the acidic air might smell new to us, but it does not surprise God. He is not huddled up right now, nervous. He's not thinking, *Oh no! I'm losing North America! What are we going to do?*

Hold this sound word. Hold this truth. God will prevail. You know whom you have believed in. God is big, and we are not. He knows what he's doing. And he has laid it out for us in his Word. We know that eventually he will punch through the darkness, tear open the sky, and return. Until then, we put one foot in front of the next, not avoiding suffering, confident of the gospel message that we preach. We share it with our neighbors, our friends, and our coworkers.

Pastor, Lead Out in Evangelism

If you are a pastor, let me help you with this. Next time you are on a plane, here's an easy script to follow with the person next to you:

You: "Are you on your way to work or are you on your way home?"

Them: "On my way home."

You: "So you were here on work?"

Them: "Yeah."

You: "What do you do?"

Them: "I'm in software sales. . . . What do you do?"

You: "I'm a pastor. So you know we have to have a conversation about Jesus, right? I mean, what kind of pastor would I be if I didn't talk to you about him?"

You know it's true. What kind of pastor would you be?

What if he puts on his headphones? Then he puts on his headphones. I'm not telling you to pull them off and say, "We're doing this!" Don't get tased by an air marshal. I'm just saying, have the courage to enter into the conversation.

Be a model for your people. It makes no sense to think of yourself as a beast in the pulpit if you are scared to death of your neighbor. And it doesn't help your church members for you to plead with them to evangelize but refuse to do it yourself.

I sometimes hear pastors say, "My primary means of evangelism is in the pulpit." Well, that might be true. But I am telling you that God gave you a neighbor. And if you are telling your people to go to their neighbors and their coworkers, you should be doing the same.

Brother pastors, we must lead out on evangelism. We must be faithful.

Conclusion

Right now, they're out there. Wherever you're from, in your city or town or neighborhood, blood-bought sons and daughters of God are out there. Jesus did not die for those who might believe. He died for those who will. So go! They *will* believe. Let's herald it. Let's tell them.

How will they believe without a preacher? I know it's scary. I know we can get rejected. I know there are ever-increasing, serious repercussions. But we must be bold. We won't regret it. There might be a cost. But ten thousand years from now, nobody will care about those costs. For we know whom we have believed in.

CHAPTER 2

The Open Door
Is the Only Door

R. Albert Mohler Jr.

Back in 2006 when we first came together for Together for the Gospel, we adopted a set of affirmations and denials. We started that statement by saying:

We are brothers in Christ united in one great cause—to stand together for the Gospel. We are convinced that the Gospel of Jesus Christ has been misrepresented, misunderstood, and marginalized in many Churches and among many who claim the name of Christ. Compromise of the Gospel has led to the preaching of false gospels, the seduction of many minds and movements, and the weakening of the Church's Gospel witness. As in previous moments of theological and spiritual crisis in the

Church, we believe that the answer to this confusion and compromise lies in a comprehensive recovery and reaffirmation of the Gospel—and in Christians banding together in Gospel Churches that display God's glory in this fallen world.

Articles IX and X in that statement are particularly important as we think about the character of the gospel and the exclusivity of the claims of Christ. *Article IX* says,

> We affirm that the Gospel of Jesus Christ is God's means of bringing salvation to His people, that sinners are commanded to believe the Gospel, and that the Church is commissioned to preach and teach the Gospel to all nations. We deny that evangelism can be reduced to any program, technique, or marketing approach. We further deny that salvation can be separated from repentance toward God and faith in our Lord Jesus Christ.

Article X goes on:

> We affirm that salvation comes to those who truly believe and confess that Jesus Christ is Lord. We deny that there is salvation in any other name, or that saving faith can take any form other than conscious belief in the Lord Jesus Christ and His saving acts.

We come together at the Together for the Gospel conference every other year to celebrate and declare that we are unashamed of the gospel. We come together to point to Christ as the door of salvation and to pray, with the apostle Paul, for an open door for the proclamation of the gospel. We also confess together that the open door is the only door. There is no other door that leads to salvation. There is no other name by which we must be saved. One door, one Lord, one faith, one baptism.

Why Declare One Door?

Several factors have made the message of the exclusivity of Christ largely unpalatable in our day.

Cultural Shift to Post-Christianity

The first is the shift to a cultural condition of post-Christianity. This, of course, doesn't mean that Christianity has disappeared. It means that Christianity, as a worldview, no longer sets the agenda for society at large. It also means that the people we meet in the community—our next-door neighbors and the parents who sit next to us at Little League games—will have a worldview that is radically different from our own.

In this cultural condition of post-Christianity, religion is increasingly seen as a mere human construct. Exclusive claims are touted as hopelessly naive, imperialistic, divisive, and dangerous. The exclusive claims of the gospel of Jesus Christ are now more shockingly out of step with our society than ever before. Today, it is not only considered bad theology, but also bad etiquette to show up believing that Jesus is the only Savior.

Generational Shift that Prizes "Etiquette"

The second issue is a generational shift that has taken place within Evangelicalism. In 1986, James Davison Hunter of the University of Virginia published a book entitled *Evangelicalism: The Coming Generation*. The generation Hunter was writing about back in 1986 is obviously no longer the coming generation. But back when it was the coming generation, Hunter pointed out that the one theological issue that was experiencing the greatest revision was the exclusivity of the gospel. Even among young evangelicals in the mid-1980s, Hunter argued that the exclusivity of the gospel presented the greatest apologetic challenge. That was almost thirty years ago.

Now we are living in a generation of young evangelicals who have been largely raised within the post-Christian intellectual condition of relativism and who have been trained in a social and cultural etiquette that doesn't allow exclusive claims because they are considered rude. Christian Smith, looking at the generation we now know as "millennials," suggested that the religion that they actually hold is "moralistic therapeutic deism." And if you hold to a moralistic therapeutic deism, it is quite obvious you're not going to hold to the exclusivity of the gospel of Jesus Christ.

In this generation, the exclusivity of the gospel is now one of the most glaringly peer-offending convictions imaginable. Just consider a young male college student from an evangelical family arriving at a major college or university campus in America. That young man and many other young men move into the dorm. One of the fellow students he meets is a Hindu freshman from India. Their conversations with one another will eventually reveal their worldviews, and their religious commitments will surface. Eventually the young man from India looks at the young evangelical and says, "Are you really telling me that my parents and all my ancestors are going to hell?" You can understand why, in that kind of cultural environment, those who call themselves evangelicals try to find a way out of the "problem" of the exclusivity of Christ.

Influence of Protestant Liberalism

A third issue is the influence of a century of Protestant Liberalism. Protestant Liberalism as far back as the late nineteenth century was, in part, a response to the problem of theological particularity. Protestant liberals sought a way out of the exclusive-truth claims of Christianity. One of the ways out was to assert that religion was simply a human construct—a human attempt to make a connection with the divine. This, of course, makes it impossible to suggest that any one religion is superior to another.

Protestant liberals felt a sense of urgency to affirm this notion because they abandoned the authority of Scripture, redefined the doctrinal character of Christianity, and transformed the gospel as it is found in the Scripture into a message of social action and personal empowerment. As they did these things, they simultaneously realized that the scandal of particularity could be eventually avoided if you simply suggested that all religions eventually led to the divine.

In liberal Protestant denominations, various forms of universalism and inclusivism have reigned for most of the last century. In the end, liberal Protestantism has settled on the notion that every belief system points to the same human quest for the divine. This led to the development of a self-declared moratorium on missions. Obviously, if you no longer believe faith comes by hearing and hearing by the word of Christ, and if you no longer believe that salvation comes only to those who come to a saving knowledge of the Lord Jesus Christ, then missions is seen as an imperialistic embarrassment. That's why Protestant liberals have basically retreated from the world for the better part of the century. In their understanding, missions are imperialism, racism, and theological hegemony.

Among the mainline Protestant denominations, universalism and inclusivism are now so settled they're no longer even controversial. There is almost a stunned surprise in those circles that anyone might still hold to the exclusivity of the gospel.

But we believe otherwise. We believe, teach, and confess that Jesus is the Savior of the world, the only Savior, the one mediator between God and sinful humanity, the sole mediator of a new and better covenant enacted on new and better promises.

The Trouble with One

One of the most controversial words you can use in any kind of setting where truth is at stake in our contemporary context is the word "one." Monotheism is really the root issue. Political philosophers increasingly suggest that the first original sin of politics and how human beings relate to one another is monotheism.

For example, Stuart Hampshire, who taught in the Ivy Leagues for many years, said that monotheism is the root evil that leads to all violence. Gore Vidal, the late novelist, said that it is the worshipers of the monotheistic sky guy with his *omnis*—omnipotence, omniscience, and so on—that led to the oppression and tyranny. If we could just rid the world of monotheism, some say, we could rid the world of all its great conflicts. In our culture, when you say one God—before you even get to one gospel—you're in trouble.

The only culturally acceptable way to hold to one God is to concede that the religions of the world are all feeble and frail human attempts to define the divine—every religion doing as best as it can. In other words, every religious system just reflects human beings' limited and ethnically determined conceptualities on their innate religious quest.

But the Christian gospel is not mere monotheism; it is a mono-redemptive message. We believe not merely that there is salvation in the name of Christ, but that there is salvation in no other name.

The Testimony of Scripture

So it should be no surprise that Jesus himself tells us about this single saving name. In the gospel of John, he says to his disciples:

"Let not your hearts be troubled. Believe in God; believe also in me. In my Father's house are many rooms. If it were not so, would I have told you that I go to prepare a place for you? And if I go and prepare a place for you, I will come again and will take you to myself, that where I am you may be also. And you know the way to where I am going." Thomas said to him, "Lord, we do not know where you are going. How can we know the way?" Jesus said to him, "I am the way, and the truth, and the life. No one comes to the Father except through me. If you had known me, you would have known my Father also. From now on you do know him and have seen him." (John 14:1–7)

John 14 is a conclusive word on the matter. Jesus is *the* way, *the* truth, *the* life. But lest there be any misunderstanding, Jesus follows that sequence with a negative assertion—"no one comes to the Father except through me." Jesus affirms and he denies. There is no way out of this text other than denying the truthfulness or authority of the text—and there are those who will do both. But we can do neither.

Jesus is preparing his disciples for his absence. He is preparing them with a promise of eternal habitation with him. And when they are with him, they will know safety, security, peace, fellowship, communion, mercy, and redemption. They will know salvation. To know Jesus is to know the way, the truth, and the life. Further, John 14:1–7 has a Trinitarian context that we cannot miss. We are not only promised that we will be with Jesus, but that we will be with the Father. Jesus makes plain that no one comes to the Father except through him.

This is clear elsewhere in the New Testament, particularly in the sequence of "I am" statements throughout the gospel of John. Consider John 10:1–11:

> "Truly, truly, I say to you, he who does not enter the sheepfold by the door but climbs in by another way, that man is a thief and a robber. But he who enters by the door is the shepherd of the sheep. To him the gatekeeper opens. The sheep hear his voice, and he calls his own sheep by name and leads them out. When he has brought out all his own, he goes before them, and the sheep follow him, for they know his voice. A stranger they will not follow, but they will flee from him, for they do not know the voice of strangers." This figure of speech Jesus used with them, but they did not understand what he was saying to them. So Jesus again said to them, "Truly, truly, I say to you, I am the door of the sheep. All who came before me are thieves and robbers, but the sheep did not listen to them. I am the door. If anyone enters by me, he will be saved and will go in and out and find pasture. The thief comes only to steal and kill and destroy. I came that they may have life and have it abundantly. I am the good shepherd. The good shepherd lays down his life for the sheep."

Likewise in John 11:17–27:

> Now when Jesus came, he found that Lazarus had already been in the tomb four days. Bethany was near Jerusalem, about two miles off, and many of the Jews had come to Martha and Mary to console them concerning their brother. So when Martha heard that Jesus was coming, she went and met him, but Mary remained seated in the house. Martha said to Jesus, "Lord, if you

had been here, my brother would not have died. But even now I know that whatever you ask from God, God will give you." Jesus said to her, "Your brother will rise again." Martha said to him, "I know that he will rise again in the resurrection on the last day." Jesus said to her, "I am the resurrection and the life. Whoever believes in me, though he die, yet shall he live, and everyone who lives and believes in me shall never die. Do you believe this?" She said to him, "Yes, Lord; I believe that you are the Christ, the Son of God, who is coming into the world."

At no point anywhere in the Scripture do we find anything other than the definite article. Never *a* Savior, but *the* Savior, *the* Christ, *the* resurrection, *the* door, *the* good Shepherd. Whenever the context is God's saving act in Christ, the definite article pertains.

Then of course, there is Acts 4:5–12:

On the next day their rulers and elders and scribes gathered together in Jerusalem, with Annas the high priest and Caiaphas and John and Alexander, and all who were of the high-priestly family. And when they had set them in the midst, they inquired, "By what power or by what name did you do this?" Then Peter, filled with the Holy Spirit, said to them, "Rulers of the people and elders, if we are being examined today concerning a good deed done to a crippled man, by what means this man has been healed, let it be known to all of you and to all the people of Israel that by the name of Jesus Christ of Nazareth, whom you crucified, whom God raised from the dead—by him this man is standing before you well. This Jesus is the stone that was rejected by you, the builders, which has become the cornerstone. And there is salvation in no one else, for there is no other name under heaven given among men by which we must be saved."

In fact these words echo what Peter had already said on the Day of Pentecost:

"Brothers, I may say to you with confidence about the patriarch David that he both died and was buried, and his tomb is with us to this day. Being therefore a prophet, and knowing that God had sworn with an oath to him that he would set one of his descendants on his throne, he foresaw and spoke about the resurrection of the Christ, that he was not abandoned to Hades, nor did his flesh see corruption. This Jesus God raised up, and of that we all are witnesses. Being therefore exalted at the right hand of God, and having received from the Father the promise of the Holy Spirit, he has poured out this that you yourselves are seeing and hearing. For David did not ascend into the heavens, but he himself says, 'The Lord said to my Lord, "Sit at my right hand, until I make your enemies your footstool."' Let all the house of Israel therefore know for certain that God has made him both Lord and Christ, this Jesus whom you crucified."

Now when they heard this they were cut to the heart, and said to Peter and the rest of the apostles, "Brothers, what shall we do?" And Peter said to them, "Repent and be baptized every one of you in the name of Jesus Christ for the forgiveness of your sins, and you will receive the gift of the Holy Spirit. For the promise is for you and for your children and for all who are far off, everyone whom the Lord our God calls to himself." And with many other words he bore witness and continued to exhort them, saying, "Save yourselves from this crooked

generation." So those who received his word were baptized, and there were added that day about three thousand souls. (Acts 2:29–41)

Peter makes clear that the promise of salvation is for all that
God calls to himself. How does he call unto himself? Only through
the Son. In other words, the open door is the only door. Christian
exclusivism is often presented as an apologetic challenge, and *it
is* an apologetic challenge because it requires the church's faithful defense and explanation. But if we see it as a negative, hard,
burdensome truth that we are forced by Christian duty to bear, we
slander the gospel. We are those who must strive to celebrate the
gospel in every dimension, even its exclusivity. The singularity of
Christ is what saves us.

The Proposal and Problem of Universalism and Inclusivism

Let's just imagine for a moment that the phenomenologists are
right and that all religions are essentially culturally conditioned
human constructs to get at the divine. Let's assume we have no
claim to privileged information and no access to revelation.

The first thing we would notice is that there is great diversity
among religions. There is Zoroastrianism, Jainism, Buddhism,
Hinduism, Islam, Baha'i, Sikhs, Aboriginal religions, ancient
paganism, New Age spirituality, various religions of the self in the
post-Christian West, Judaism, and Christianity. It's a long catalog
and we've just scratched the surface.

Many argue that the similarities far outweigh the differences.
Most have holy books. All have religious teachers. All promise
blessings to their adherents. Most require some obedience to a law
or liturgy or lifestyle. But at that point the commonalities end. In
their essences, each religion is radically different. They're not even

all theistic. Buddhism is not clearly theistic. Hinduism is clearly polytheistic. Those that are theistic to some degree are at odds over the character of God. Is God's character good or evil, or some combination of the two? Are there both good and evil gods? Does God speak? In what form does he speak? Does he reveal himself in words, or in riddles and puzzles?

These various religions don't share common ground on human origins. They do not share common ground on what it means to be human. They do not share common ground on the nature of the problem facing humanity. They disagree on the meaning of history, on what is required of humanity, on who can save us, and on the issue of where history is headed. In other words, you can only argue that these religions are virtually the same if you don't actually know anything about them.

Liberal Protestantism says we should celebrate diversity and allow everyone to find his own way. They claim we should forfeit claims of Christian exclusivism—forgo conversions and missionary ambition. The liberal Protestant world is now settled into some form of consensus that includes universalism and inclusivism. Universalism simply says everyone will eventually be accepted, regardless of any disposition or morality or whether they hear any gospel and believe it. More common amongst most Christian denominations, even those marked by Protestant liberalism, is a form of inclusivism that claims that all these faith systems eventually represent the same thing, but that at the end of the day the decisive teacher will be discovered to have been Jesus Christ.

Now think with me for a moment about Roman Catholicism. Prior to Vatican II, what characterized the official teaching of the Roman Catholic Church was that which was defined by Cyprian in the early church: *extra ecclesiam nulla salus*—outside the church, there is no salvation. But Vatican II represented a massive theological transformation in Catholicism In Vatican II, the church declared:

> All this holds true not only for Christians, but for all men of good will in whose hearts grace works in an unseen way. For, since Christ died for all men, and since the ultimate vocation of man is in fact one, and divine, we ought to believe that the Holy Spirit in a manner known only to God offers to every man the possibility of being associated with this paschal mystery.

At many points and in several documents of Vatican II, the church officially stated a position of inclusivism, and not only that, but a radical inclusivism that said persons should actually be understood, no matter their religion, as being drawn into the saving work of Christ.

The most radical proponent of this was Pope John Paul II. In 1979, in his encyclical *Redemptor Hominis,* he wrote: "Man—every man without exception whatever—has been redeemed by Christ . . . because with man—with each man without any exception whatever—Christ is in a way united, even when man is unaware of it." The Roman Catholic Church officially teaches inclusivism as the means, and that means universalism as the end.

An advisor to Vatican II, a German theologian by the name of Karl Rahner, suggested that Christians should understand the adherents of other world religions as, "anonymous Christians." He argued, "Christianity does not simply confront the member of an extra-Christian religion as a mere non-Christian, but as someone who can and must already be regarded in this or that respect as an anonymous Christian." Likewise he argued, "The church will not so much regard herself today as the exclusive community of those who have a claim to salvation, but rather as the historically tangible vanguard and the historically and socially constituted explicit expression of what the Christian hopes is present as a hidden reality even outside the visible church."[9]

It would be very convenient if this were true. This would relieve an awful lot of pressure on us because when we see an adherent of a non-Christian religion, we can simply rest in the knowledge that they are actually "anonymous Christians." The freshman in the dorm with the Hindu roommate would find himself in a much less awkward situation if he could simply consider his new friend an "anonymous Christian."

And of course if the world is made up of "anonymous Christians" then there really aren't any unreached people groups! There are just people groups made up of people who are anonymous Christians. Our task is merely to go and declare to them that they are Christians, even though they do not know it yet.

There's only one problem with this: the absolute absence of any anonymous Christian in the New Testament, and the clear teaching of Christ and of the apostles that faith comes by hearing and hearing by the word of Christ. The Scripture is very clear. If they do not hear, they will not believe, and if they do not believe, they will not be saved.

But it's not just the Roman Catholic Church that has adopted universalism. Even some who have identified with Evangelicalism have adopted it. Consider Rob Bell's book *Love Wins* or Brian McLaren's *A Generous Orthodoxy*. McLaren writes:

> I don't believe making disciples must equal making
> adherents to the Christian religion. It may be advisable in
> many (not all!) circumstances to help people become fol-
> lowers of Jesus and remain within their Buddhist, Hindu,
> or Jewish contexts.[10]

All that stands between that statement and the truth is the New Testament. We need to recognize as we consider this question that the theological cost of surrendering the singularity of Christ is more massive than many may understand. John Hick, who was the leading proponent in the twentieth century of what he called "the non-absoluteness of Christianity," said that Christianity, in order to adopt a posture of non-absoluteness, would have to give up the doctrine of the Trinity, the deity of Christ, the claim of incarnation, and substitutionary atonement. In other words, it would have to cease being Christianity.

Only Jesus Will Do

Frankly, all of these proposals work fine if we don't need a Savior. But we do. And there is only one Savior, and salvation is in his name alone. He is the only Savior, the sole mediator, the Christ, the Son of the Living God, the Way, the Truth, and the Life, the Resurrection, and the Redeemer. If all we need is a teacher of enlightenment, the Buddha will do. If all we need is a collection of gods for every occasion, Hinduism will do. If all we need is a tribal deity, any tribal deity will do. If all we need is a lawgiver, Moses will do. If all we need is a set of rules and a way of devotion, Mohammad or Joseph Smith will do. If all we need is inspiration and insight into the sovereign self, Oprah will do. But if we need a Savior, only Jesus will do.

That is why we are unashamed of the gospel. With the apostle Paul, we declare to all peoples everywhere that it is the power of God unto salvation for all who believe, to the Jew first, and also to the Gentile. That's why we are not ashamed of the gospel. In it is the power of God unto salvation.

The open door is the only door—but the only door is an *open door*! We declare Christ as Savior and Lord, the one who died on the cross and was buried and was raised on the third day by the power of God. We declare salvation to all who call upon the name of the Lord, who hear the gospel and believe, and by believing are saved.

We declare Christ as the Savior of the world, eagerly preaching this gospel of salvation to the entire world, knowing that the Father is calling to himself men and women from every tongue, tribe, people, and nation. This is not the burden we bear or the apologetic challenge that hinders us. This is the good news of salvation.

We need a Savior and, thankfully, Jesus is that savior. God so loved the world that he sent his only begotten Son that whosoever believes in him might not perish but have everlasting life (see John 3:16). The open door is the only door, and the only door is an open door. There is salvation in this name and in no other name. Jesus is the Way, the Truth, and the Life. No one comes to the Father but by him. He is the resurrection and the life. To come to him is to find that life. This is the gospel of which we are unashamed, and this is the gospel in which we stand together.

CHAPTER 3

The Pathology of Counterfeit Faith
(John 6)

John MacArthur

I grew up in a pastor's house. My father loved the Lord, the Bible, and the church. The congregation he pastored was a typical revivalistic fundamental church, and I assumed that everyone in it was saved. I assumed that if you walked an aisle, signed a card, or prayed a prayer you were a believer. However, in high school I began to question the salvation of certain people in the church. Their lives did not bear testimony to what they professed. I knew there was something more to Christianity than what I saw in these people, but I didn't know where to find it.

No Category for Apostasy

Then, I found some mystical books. As early as junior high, I was reading things like *The Imitation of Life* and books by Ian Bounds. I was reading about people who got on their knees and wore grooves in the floor with their prayer life—and I wondered where this real spirituality was.

I was raised with what you might call *decisional evangelism*—with its practices like the raising of hands, the walking of aisles, the kneeling on benches—and a very undefined doctrine of salvation, justification, and sanctification. I watched people whose lives caused doubt in my mind as to their true salvation. This doubt led to certainty when I witnessed them leave the church.

One of those people was a close friend and fellow teammate in high school, Ralph. He and I used to go down to Pershing Square in the city of Los Angeles and witness to people. We graduated together, and then he went to college and declared himself an atheist. I didn't have a category for Ralph.

I went to college and I had a buddy there, a co-captain of the football team; his name was Don. He and I led a Bible study together. He was headed for seminary, but then Don did a PhD in philosophy instead, denied the faith, and was arrested for lewd conduct. I really didn't have a category for Don.

When I went to seminary I had another friend, the son of one of the leading faculty members. After he graduated, he set up a Buddhist altar in his house. I didn't understand that.

When I came to my final year in seminary I had to pick a thesis subject. It seemed there was no other choice for me, so I wrote on Judas, because I couldn't understand Judas either. I couldn't understand how Judas, after three years of being in the presence of Christ, could walk away from Christ and betray him. I couldn't understand anyone who walked away from Christ.

I remember watching the rapid growth of the Billy Graham Organization. I remember watching those crusades all over the world with people pouring down aisles but never showing up in churches afterwards. The organization confessed that they weren't sure how many of those people were really converted.

Reaching the Reached or Evangelizing the Church

I came to Grace Community Church after seminary and I was still burdened by this topic. On my first Sunday at Grace—February 9, 1969—my sermon was on Matthew 7:21–23: "Not everyone who says to Me, 'Lord, Lord,' will enter the kingdom of heaven" (v. 21).[11] Within months it became evident that there were elders, deacons, choir members, and all kinds of people in the church who didn't know the Lord.

One year after that, a book came out written by the rather eccentric theologian John Warwick Montgomery called *Damned through the Church*. He chronicled the history of heresy, which had affected the church and damned people in the church. This reinforced my thinking that there were nonbelievers in the church.

So I began to realize very early in my ministry that I needed to do the work of an evangelist *in* the church. When Paul wrote to Timothy, he instructed him, with emphasis, "Do the work of an evangelist, fulfill your ministry" (2 Tim. 4:5). Someone has to reach the unreached; I began trying to reach the reached.

I began to question things like the *Four Laws Book*—that Jesus is "Savior" but not Lord. I began to question carnal Christianity. I wrote a little book called *Kingdom Living Here and Now and the Beatitudes,* which upset a lot of people. I wrote another book called *The Gospel According to Jesus,* addressing the issue of genuine salvation, and another one called *The Gospel According to the*

Apostles, followed by *Ashamed of the Gospel, The Truth War, Hard to Believe,* and *The Jesus You Can't Ignore.*

I think the Lord has shaped me to evangelize the church. Not many people realize that aspect of evangelism. I know I didn't, since I grew up with the assumption that if you walked an aisle and prayed a prayer, you were in, regardless of what your life was like. But now I know that the church contains false converts. Let me tell you something, hell will be far worse for the reached people than it will ever be for the unreached. And I fear that the failure to confront people on this issue is more common today in churches that feature a cheap gospel and a glitzy–pop Jesus, and whose congregations are neither regularly confronted about the legitimacy of their profession nor regularly warned about the most eternally devastating of all sins—knowing the gospel and walking away. So maybe that helps explain my ministry a little bit and why I always seem to be burdened to correct gospel errors that infect the church. Maybe I'm just an evangelist to the church. This seems to be an emphasis that God has laid on my heart.

God wants believers to have confidence in their salvation. We read in Hebrews 10:19–22, "Therefore, brethren, since we have confidence to enter the holy place by the blood of Jesus, by a new and living way which He inaugurated for us through the veil, that is, His flesh, and since we have a great priest over the house of God, let us draw near with a sincere heart in full assurance of faith." The author of Hebrews also writes, "Let us hold fast the confession of our hope without wavering, . . . let us consider how to stimulate one another to love and good deeds, not forsaking our own assembling together, as is the habit of some, but encouraging one another; and all the more as you see the day drawing near" (10:23–25). The "day drawing near" means judgment. As a result, Christians should be confident in their salvation, since if you're not genuine you're going to get caught in that judgment.

I appreciate what John Piper has said before—if you don't pursue holiness in your life, you're going to hell. In my experience it is the most heartbreaking part of pastoral ministry to see someone walk away from Christ. I can deal with the dying children; I can deal with the broken hearts of people who lose a spouse or a child; I can deal with all the diseases; I can deal with all the struggles of life. But there is a profound pain in my heart when somebody just turns his or her back on Christ and walks away. It's not rare; I deal with it all the time. It is, I fear, the eternal undoing of all the hope and all the warnings that we've tried to give, sometimes for years and years.

Counterfeits

Jesus experienced this as well. We read in John 6:

> Therefore many of His disciples, when they heard this said, "This is a difficult statement; who can listen to it?" But Jesus, conscious that His disciples grumbled at this, said to them, "Does this cause you to stumble? What then if you see the Son of Man ascending to where He was before? It is the Spirit who gives life; the flesh profits nothing; the words that I have spoken to you are spirit and are life. But there are some of you who do not believe." For Jesus knew from the beginning who they were who did not believe, and who it was who would betray Him. And He was saying, "For this reason I have said to you, that no one can come to Me unless it has been granted him from the Father." As a result of this many of His disciples withdrew and were not walking with Him anymore. (vv. 60–66)

We continue reading in verses 67–71:

So Jesus said to the twelve, "You do not want to go away also, do you?" Simon Peter answered Him, "Lord, to whom shall we go? You have the words of eternal life. We have believed and have come to know that you are the holy one of God." Jesus answered them, "Did I Myself not choose you, the twelve, and yet one of you is a devil?" Now He meant Judas the son of Simon Iscariot, for he, one of the twelve, was going to betray Him.

Look again at verse 66, "As a result of this many of His disciples withdrew and were not walking with Him anymore." That is very strong language. In the original language it expresses finality. The same idea appears in Luke 9:62, "No one, after putting his hand to the plow and looking back, is fit for the kingdom of God." What is tragic about this incident in Jesus' life is that there are disciples that walk away. John later describes such false followers who abandon the Lord Jesus in his first epistle: "They went out from us, but they were not really of us; for if they had been of us, they would have remained with us; but they went out so that it would be shown that they all are not of us" (1 John 2:19).

We're familiar with that verse. But are we aware of the verse that precedes it? First John 2:18 calls these apostates anti-Christs. Some people will defect from Christ in their heart, and we won't know until the judgment reveals it. It will be revealed for some on that day as Matthew 13:24–30 illustrates that the angels, who are at the behest of God, separate the wheat from the tares. Until that day we may not know who the false disciples are, but sadly there are many cases we do know of.

I've pastored Grace Community Church since 1969, and I have stayed long enough to see the fruitless soil that looked good for a season. As our Lord says in Luke 8:13, "They believe for a while." I have seen them come and go—from the most faithful loving congregation, under the most firm and clear biblical preaching—the half-converted who can't handle any tribulation, who can't loosen their grip on sin, who can't let go of the world, who can't let go of money, who can't let go of the culture. I have reminded them through the years repeatedly of 1 Corinthians 10:1–12, the example of unfaithful Israel in the desert, "Let him who thinks he stands take heed lest he fall" (v. 12). I have cried out to them from Colossians 1 that, "Yes, the work of Christ on the cross is applied to you if you remain faithful" (my paraphrase). Every time I have called them to the Lord's Table, hundreds and hundreds of times through the years, I have asked them to examine themselves because a man must examine himself.

I have poured out my heart from 2 Corinthians 13:5, "Test yourselves to see if you are in the faith." I have gone through the warnings of Hebrews in chapters 2, 3, 4, and 6. "How will we escape if we neglect so great a salvation?" (2:3). If it was horrendous for those who ignored the law, what's it going to be for those who ignore the gospel? I have reminded them so often of Hebrews 10:23, of how important it is to hold fast the confession of our hope without wavering. God will be faithful, but you must hold fast the confession. Then I've reminded them of Hebrews 10:26, which is the reality of apostasy, "For if we go on sinning willfully after receiving the knowledge of the truth, there no longer remains a sacrifice for sins." What is apostasy? It is going on in the unbroken pattern of corrupt sinfulness after receiving the knowledge of the truth. That's the fact of apostasy.

The Consequences of Apostasy

What is the result of apostasy? There's no remaining sacrifice for sin. There is only a "terrifying expectation of judgment, and the fury of a fire that will consume the adversaries" (Heb. 10:27). Hebrews 10:29 says, "How much severer punishment do you think he will deserve who has trampled under foot the Son of God, and has regarded as unclean the blood of the covenant by which he was sanctified, and has insulted the Spirit of grace?" The writer of Hebrews wrote this to an assembly of people who constituted a church, and I don't know stronger words than that to say to a church.

What are the results of apostasy? Unparalleled punishment in hell. The Lord will judge his people. You know why Jeremiah wails with tears? Do you know why Jesus weeps over Israel in Luke 19? Because those who have the greatest spiritual privilege suffer the greatest eternal punishment, if they reject it. That is why Hebrews 10:31 is a message for the church: "It is a terrifying thing to fall into the hands of the living God." Especially terrifying if you know the truth. Verses 35 and 36 sum it up: "Therefore, do not throw away your confidence, which has a great reward. For you have need of endurance, so that when you have done the will of God, you may receive what was promised." You need endurance and perseverance, so that when you have done the will of God, you may receive what was promised. Do you know how to get what was promised in eternity? Endure! Persevere and do the will of God. False disciples shrink back to eternal destruction; true disciples persevere in faith to the end. I don't know if you preach that way in your church, but you should.

The Characteristics of False Disciples

This paradigm of true and false discipleship will be evident as we survey John 6, which is such a powerful, sorrowful, and poignant text. Let's begin by reading verse 66 again: "As a result of this many of His disciples withdrew, and were not walking with

Him anymore." What's the pathology of this? How does this happen? To answer these questions, let's look at the character of false disciples.

Everything really began at the beginning of the chapter, at the miracle meal. All four Gospels record this historical event, which caps off the Galilean ministry and is the most extensive miracle Jesus did in terms of the number of people who participated. It's one thing to heal a blind man and a deaf person; it's something else to feed twenty thousand to twenty-five thousand people who all participated in the miracle. Matthew wrote that Jesus, "seeing the people, . . . felt compassion for them, because they were distressed and dispirited like sheep without a shepherd" (9:36). Jesus' heart must have been overwhelmed with joy. It all started so wonderfully, but we begin to see the pattern of false disciples form right there in the high moment of that day.

Attracted by the Crowd

The first thing to note is that false disciples are attracted by a crowd. Most people follow a crowd even when they have no idea what the crowd is there for. What do you do when you see a crowd? Go the other way? I don't think so. What do people do driving down the highway when they see a crowd of people off the road? They slow down and sometimes even stop. We're naturally drawn by a crowd. Crowds have an energy of their own, whether it's a spontaneous incident that has drawn people, a rock concert, or a megachurch. The anonymity of crowds, the excitement, the energy, the interest—it becomes attractive to people with mundane lives. You could say the bigger the crowd the more likely you are to attract people who are only drawn by the crowd.

Fascinated by the Supernatural

The second point to note is that false disciples can be fascinated by the supernatural. I think our whole culture is bizarre, because they're so caught up in the supernatural. I have no interest in that. I can't watch anything on television but news or a sporting event, because I can't live in the fantasy world. I can't live with weird unreal beings that dominate television. There's a fascinating escape mentality in our culture, the enthrallment with the supernatural. Likewise, people in the ancient world would be fascinated by the prospect of something miraculous. People are still intrigued by the promise of the paranormal even from people who can't pull it off—fake miracle workers. But in John 6 we see the real deal. Jesus' power over demons, disease, death, and nature was fascinating because such things had never happened in the history of the world.

Just think about Jesus' power manifested in that one miracle. I asked a scientist in our church, "How much power would it take to make a half-pound meal for twenty thousand people?" He went back, calculated it, and came to me and said, "All the electrical power on earth operating at 100 percent output for 100 percent of the time for four thousand years." That's pretty good, but that was no big deal for Jesus. Why? Because He created the sun. The sun consumes approximately six hundred million tons of matter per second, generating enough energy in that one second to supply all the U.S. energy needs for thirteen billion years. That did not come from some oozing mud with an amoeba in it; it came from the Creator of the universe—the same Creator who fed that large group of people.

The display of power drew these massive crowds, because people are attracted to supernatural wonders. Simon Magus was even willing to pay for it (see Acts 8:9–24). The pull is so strong toward the supernatural that even the false miracle workers can draw and deceive crowds. False disciples are fascinated by the miraculous.

Hungry for Worldly Benefits

A third characteristic of a false disciple is evident in John 6:14–15:

> Therefore when the people saw the sign which He had performed, they said, "This is truly the Prophet who is to come into the world." So Jesus, perceiving that they were intending to come and take Him by force to make Him king, withdrew again to the mountain by Himself alone.

False disciples crave worldly benefits.

The people want to make Jesus king. This is carnal enthusiasm. This is free food permanently. What Jesus had done was a taste of what he could continue to do. The crowd had a desire for comfort, desire for provision, desire for freedom from the difficulty of the battle for bread. "What can he do for us?"—that's what was in the minds of the people. This is the same kind of thinking that accompanies the prosperity gospel, for the prosperity gospel works on natural desire.

We see the crowd become bold and demanding to Jesus in John 6:28: "What shall we do, so that we may work the works of God?" I don't know if you're aware of what they're asking, but this is not a spiritual question. They're saying to Jesus, "Give us the power," similar to what Simon Magus said in Acts 8:19. The people want to be able to speak these things into existence. They want to be able to create their own world, to create their own fulfillment. They want to be miracle workers.

Jesus responds in John 6:29, "This is the work of God, that you believe in Him whom He has sent." In other words, Jesus is saying, "The only participation you'll ever have in a miracle is the miracle of believing in him whom he sent." We must remember that miracles were confined to Jesus and the apostles, but Jesus is saying that there is a miracle you can participate in, there is a work of God that you can partake in; it's faith and believing. Jesus repeatedly called the crowds to believe. We see this in John 6:47, "Truly, truly, I say to you, he who believes has eternal life."

Let's recap. The people demand, "Give us the power." Jesus responds, "You're not going to get the power. The only participation you'll have in the power of God, the only time you'll be engaged in the work of God, is when you believe on him whom he sent." So they said to him, "If you're not going to give us the power, then what are you going to do for a sign, so that we may see and believe you? What work do you perform?" (John 6:30, my paraphrase). Since Jesus isn't going to give the people the power, they're still expecting him to give them the provisions. They want Jesus to keep doing what they want him to do.

You might say, "That's bizarre, because he just created a meal. Does he have to validate himself?" The people diminished the miracle Jesus had just performed: "Our fathers ate manna in the wilderness; as it is written, 'He gave them bread out of heaven, to eat'" (6:31). It's as if their response is, "Moses provided food for many years. If you want to prove to us that you're a prophet, one miracle isn't going to do it. You must give us this bread constantly."

Then we read in verse 34, "Lord, always give us this bread." This is the pattern of the false disciple: drawn by the crowd, fascinated by the supernatural, sees a means to have his personal temporal desires fulfilled, and consequently makes demands on God and expects God to validate who he is by meeting their demands.

No Interest in the Person of Jesus

The fourth characteristic of false disciples is that they have no real interest in the Lord Jesus. We skipped a little section from John 6:16–21 of Jesus walking on the water overnight. The response of the individuals in the boat is recorded in Matthew 14:33. Matthew writes, "And those who were in the boat worshiped Him, saying, 'You are certainly God's Son!'" The true disciples acknowledged who Jesus was. They had an interest in the Lord Jesus. They were the people described in the parable found in Matthew 13:44–46, individuals who sold all to buy the field in order to obtain the treasure; those who sold all their possessions to buy the pearl of great price.

However, the crowd in John 6 has no interest in Jesus. Jesus said in John 6:35–36, "I am the bread of life; he who comes to Me will not hunger, and he who believes in Me will never thirst. But I said to you that you have seen Me, and yet you do not believe." This is the issue. Sure, these disciples are attracted by the crowds. Of course they're fascinated by the supernatural. Yes, they want power and provision—miracle power and all the provision they can get to satisfy their carnal desires. But they have no interest in Christ as the bread of life. No soul interest in him whatsoever.

Jesus continued this discussion regarding the bread of life in verse 51: "I am the living bread that came down out of heaven; if anyone eats of this bread, he will live forever; and the bread also which I will give for the life of the world is My flesh." Jesus is saying, "You have to eat my flesh and drink my blood." This is atonement; it's now about sin, repentance, substitution, imputation, and personal appropriation of this truth. A true disciple must embrace the cross. Yet, these disciples have no interest in Christ or the cross.

The cross is an offense, and it is a stumbling block. Here's the pathology that we've thus addressed in our text: false disciples are drawn by the crowd, fascinated by the prospect of the supernatural, desire worldly benefits, and have no true interest in Christ, completely rejecting the notion of atonement.

Verse 59 clarifies that this incident took place as Jesus taught in the synagogue in Capernaum. Remember what Jesus said about Capernaum in Matthew 11:23–24: "And you, Capernaum, will not be exalted to heaven, will you? You will descend to Hades; for if the miracles had occurred in Sodom which occurred in you, it would have remained to this day. Nevertheless I say to you it will be more tolerable." It will be more tolerable for the homosexuals in Sodom who tried to rape angels than it will be for the religious Jews in Capernaum who rejected Jesus Christ.

Mass Defection

The defection in this narrative comes fast: "Therefore many of His disciples, when they heard this said, 'This is a difficult statement'" (John 6:60)—*a hard teaching* most translations say. "Who can listen to it?" Figuratively, the word used for *difficult* means unpleasant, objectionable, offensive, unacceptable, harsh, violent, fierce, defiant, or repulsive. The bottom line, the NASB says, is that this is a difficult statement—but please give me more than that. The text is not claiming that this statement is confusing to them; it's crystal clear to them. One lexicon states that the term *Sklēros* used figuratively means "grating on the mind." What irritated them? Jesus said he came down from heaven. He said he is the only true food for eternal life. He said he would die as an atonement and a sacrifice for sinners. That's a very grating message. Nothing that Jesus did offended them, because everything he said offended them.

Based on Jesus' miracles the people were willing to declare him a prophet. Nicodemus said this on behalf of those who were not true believers in John 3:2: "We know that You have come from God as a teacher." But that's not enough. Jesus didn't claim to only be a teacher come from God, he claimed to be God. He claimed to be eternal, from heaven, the source of life, the Son of Man, the Son of God, the One who alone grants eternal life, the One who personally raises the dead, and the One who provides atonement for sin. All this from the mouth of a local carpenter from Nazareth who looked just like everyone else.

The Rejection of Words

The issue the crowd had with Jesus was not associated with his actions, but with his words. Sometimes you hear this crazy statement: "Preach the gospel and, if necessary, use words." I don't know who said that. And I don't want to give tribute to the wrong person, because it's so stupid. You can't preach the gospel without words. That's a lie. Preach the gospel and always use words. Of course, people welcome you when you feed them. Of course, they welcome you when you give them medicine and you heal them. But don't be under the delusion that because people welcome you when you give them what they want they will respond when you call them to repentance and faith.

They will not reject you for your works, but they will reject you for your words. You still do the works, but don't assume there's an immediate connection. Read what Jesus said in John 8:31–32: "So Jesus was saying to those Jews who had believed Him, 'If you continue in My word, then you are truly disciples of Mine; and you will know the truth, and the truth will make you free.'"

As Jesus spoke these things some people believed, but further into the chapter we learn more about them, "I know you were Abraham's descendants; yet you seek to kill Me, because My word has no place in you. I speak the things which I have seen with My Father; therefore you also do the things which you heard from your father" (8:37–38). It comes all the way down to Jesus saying, "You are of your father the devil" (8:44).

Then we read in verse 45, "But because I speak the truth, you do not believe Me"—and verse 47, "He who is of God hears the words of God." We are reminded in Luke 4:16–30 that Jesus went back to the Nazareth synagogue he grew up in to preach the gospel, to fulfill Isaiah 61. He said, "The gospel is for the poor, the prisoners, the blind and oppressed" (my paraphrase). His words so offended them that by the time he was done they tried to throw him off a cliff and kill him.

People want the miracles, but the words will kill you. In John 7:1, at the end of the verse the Jews are seeking to kill Jesus. In John 8:59, they picked up stones to throw at him, and it's always because of his words. In John 6:61 we read, "But Jesus, conscious that His disciples grumbled at this, said to them, 'Does this cause you to stumble?'" Well of course they stumbled, because his words were a stumbling block.

But Jesus' words also contain life. He says, "It is the Spirit who gives life; the flesh profits nothing; the words that I have spoken to you are spirit and are life" (6:63). If you're going to do evangelism, you have to speak the words of the gospel, just like Jesus did:

"If anyone keeps My word he will never see death." (John 8:51)

"He who rejects Me and doesn't receive My sayings, has one who judges him; the word I spoke is what will judge him at the last day." (John 12:48)

"If you keep My commandments, you will abide in My love." (John 15:10)

"These things I have spoken to you so that My joy may be in you, and that your joy may be made full." (John 15:11)

Salvation is about believing the words. Faith comes by hearing (Rom. 10:17), hearing the message concerning Christ. The issue is described in John 6:64, "'But there are some of you who do not believe.' For Jesus knew from the beginning who they were who did not believe, and who it was that would betray Him." What fascinates me about this narrative is that Jesus knew from the beginning who wouldn't believe and yet he pled with all of them to believe. In John 8:21–24 Jesus said, "If you don't believe you'll die in your sins and where I go you'll never come" (my paraphrase). I also love Jesus' plea for them to stay in John 6:62; it's as if Jesus is saying, "Why don't you just hang around until the ascension? Wouldn't you just please stay until the ascension? I'm telling you, I came from heaven. If you stay you'll see me go back. Then you'll know. Stay" (my paraphrase).

We continue reading in John 6:66, "As a result of this [this kind of talk, this message, these words] many of His disciples withdrew and were not walking with Him anymore." The result was unbelief, an unwillingness to hear and to believe the words from heaven they had heard. The crowd abandoned the Lord Jesus Christ due to their worldly interests. They left for good. They went out. That's the false disciples.

True Followers

Look at John 6:67–69 for the description of a true disciple. Brokenhearted Jesus—crushed, maybe even weeping—sat with the few who remained. Pensive, exhausted, and disappointed out of his pain, he said, "You do not want to go away also, do you?" (v. 67). Simon Peter, the spokesman, answered him: "Lord, to whom shall we go? You have words of eternal life. We have believed and have come to know that You are the Holy One of God" (vv. 68–69).

By the way, "the Holy One of God" was one of Isaiah's favorite names for God. And now in the incarnation it becomes the name of Christ. Peter was saying, "We know who you are. We know you're the Christ, the Son of God. We know you're the Holy One of God."

True discipleship affirms faith in all the claims and all the truths that Jesus has ever made. These disciples are the ones who receive eternal life. What a precious moment we witness in this text—true believers affirming their commitment to Christ. However, we're not allowed to dwell on the blessed confession very long because we're back into the pathos that dominates the text—the tragedy of false discipleship and mass defection. "'Did I Myself not choose you, the twelve, and yet one of you is a devil?' Now He meant Judas the son of Simon Iscariot, for he, one of the twelve, was going to betray Him" (John 6:70–71).

This is not intended to open up a biographical study of Judas, but only to make the final point of the whole chapter: expect anti-Christs and devils among those you disciple. Judas wouldn't even be exposed for another six months. And he was so good at his hypocrisy that when Jesus said one of the twelve was a traitor, they all thought it might be them.

Contrasting Examples

Two names appear at the end of John 6, Peter and Judas. Both were drawn to Jesus. Both were personally called by Jesus. Both were taught by Jesus. Both affirmed devotion to Jesus. Both were trained for ministry by Jesus and did ministry alongside Jesus. Both taught Scripture. Both were taught Scripture in Jesus' small group. Both experienced the gripping evidence of our Lord's heavenly perfection. Both saw the miracles of Jesus. Both heard the Lord Jesus answer every theological question truthfully, completely, and clearly. Both were daily confronted with the nature of sin, death, judgment, and the need for repentance and grace. Both were told of the reality of hell and heaven. Both even preached the Lord Jesus as the Son of God, Messiah, and Savior. Both knew their sinfulness. Both experienced overwhelming guilt. Both gave themselves to Satan. Both took sides against the Lord. Both betrayed the Lord Jesus boldly, emphatically, and openly. Both were devastated by their betrayal. Both felt guilty about it.

However, one is considered so honorable that in spite of his betrayal some of you are named after him. The other one is so dishonorable that none of you are named after him. One ended a manic suicide. The other is a martyred saint. Both were sorry, but what was the major difference? For Peter, the words of Jesus were life. He received them, he believed them, he obeyed them, he rejoiced in them, and eventually he preached them.

For Judas, the words were death. They killed his interest. They killed his ambition. They devastated his expectations. They overwhelmed him with angry resentment. It's always about the words. Therefore, warning the people in the church is serious business in evangelism. There is far greater punishment in hell for the reached than the unreached.

Peace amidst Defection

What does Jesus turn to in the midst of such defection? He turns to the only place any of us can: "This is the reason I have said to you, that no one can come to Me unless it has been granted him from the Father" (John 6:65). Jesus had declared this truth earlier in the chapter:

> "All that the Father gives Me will come to Me, and the
> one who comes to Me I will certainly not cast out. For
> I have come down from heaven, not to do My own will,

but the will of Him who sent Me. This is the will of Him who sent Me, that of all that He has given Me I lose nothing, but raise it up on the last day." (John 6:37–39)

Where did Jesus find his rest? He found his rest in the sovereign elective purposes of God. Without that truth I don't think I could be in pastoral ministry, because I would tend to lay the failure at my own feet.

"No one can come to Me unless the Father who sent Me draws him; and I will raise him up on the last day" (John 6:44). I find my rest in the same place that the original Calvinist found his rest—in God's sovereignty. This would have been a perfect moment for Jesus to harmonize human responsibility and divine sovereignty, and yet he doesn't say a word. He just leaves it there. How do I find peace in the midst of the defection? I rest in the purpose of God.

Grace be with all those who love our Lord Jesus Christ with an incorruptible love. Amen.

CHAPTER 4

The Happiness of Heaven in the Repentance of Sinners
(Luke 15)

Thabiti Anyabwile

"Unashamed." That's the theme of this book. But stop for a minute. How many of us feel unashamed when we think of our lives of personal evangelism?

Every preacher should be a man of integrity. When he proclaims God's Word he should do so with an honest and humble heart.

For that to be true of me, I must begin by confessing. I am not the greatest evangelist in the world. I am not the greatest evangelist in this multi-authored book. I am not the greatest evangelist in my present or any past church. If I were in a room by myself, I'm not sure that I would be the greatest evangelist in the room!

I do the work of an evangelist. And I do it happily, but far too infrequently. I'm learning something about my heart. I suffer from two afflictions. Perhaps you can identify. First, I don't care enough about the lost. I do care, but my concern and love for the lost are not yet at the driving, animating level that prompts more zealous personal evangelism. Second, there's a defect in my approach to evangelism.

Perhaps this second affliction deserves a little more explanation. In his 1970 book called *Today's Gospel: Authentic or Synthetic?*, Walter J. Chantry writes,

> In the twentieth century the church has tried to see how little it could say and still get converts. The assumption has been that a minimal message will conserve our forces, spread the Gospel farther, and, of course, preserve a unity among evangelicals. It has succeeded in spreading the truth so thinly that the world cannot see it. Four facts droned over and over have bored sinners around us and weakened the church as well.[12]

All of my life has been lived in the wake of Chantry's words. I came to faith in and have lived my Christian life in an era largely characterized by a doctrinally light and sudden-conversion focused form of evangelism. Which means, I'm having to overcome certain attitudes, beliefs, and approaches to evangelism that are well-intended but perhaps not so biblical. I notice that I can shrink back and grimace when it comes to sharing the "hard parts" of the gospel, like the call to repentance. Repentance can be a footnote, a passing mention, in many of the gospel conversations I have.

I don't think I'm alone in this. When major televangelists— televangelists!—appear on national talk shows and downplay the importance of sin and hell, then there's bound to be a weakness in our evangelism. When major Christian leaders look for a way to accommodate certain sinful lifestyles without calling for repentance, then something has gone wrong not just with *my* evangelistic efforts but with that of many others.

Here's the problem I want to address in this chapter: *if we get the motive and method of evangelism wrong, we will find ourselves betraying the very motive and method of heaven.*

And here's the main point I want to make drawing from Luke 15: *when it comes to evangelism, nothing is more important to emphasize and more joy-producing in heaven than the sinner's repentance.* Understanding why heaven rejoices in the repentance of sinners helps me with timidity and impatience with the "hard parts" of evangelism. It helps me to be unashamed.

Start by reading Luke 15:

> Now the tax collectors and sinners were all drawing near to hear him. And the Pharisees and the scribes grumbled, saying, "This man receives sinners and eats with them."
>
> So he told them this parable: "What man of you, having a hundred sheep, if he has lost one of them, does not leave the ninety-nine in the open country, and go after the one that is lost, until he finds it? And when he has found it, he lays it on his shoulders, rejoicing. And when he comes home, he calls together his friends and his neighbors, saying to them, 'Rejoice with me, for I have found my sheep that was lost.' Just so, I tell you, there will be more joy in heaven over one sinner who repents than over ninety-nine righteous persons who need no repentance.
>
> "Or what woman, having ten silver coins, if she loses one coin, does not light a lamp and sweep the house and seek diligently until she finds it? And when she has found it, she calls together her friends and neighbors,

saying, 'Rejoice with me, for I have found the coin that I had lost.' Just so, I tell you, there is joy before the angels of God over one sinner who repents."

And he said, "There was a man who had two sons. And the younger of them said to his father, 'Father, give me the share of property that is coming to me.' And he divided his property between them. Not many days later, the younger son gathered all he had and took a journey into a far country, and there he squandered his property in reckless living. And when he had spent everything, a severe famine arose in that country, and he began to be in need. So he went and hired himself out to one of the citizens of that country, who sent him into his fields to feed pigs. And he was longing to be fed with the pods that the pigs ate, and no one gave him anything.

"But when he came to himself, he said, 'How many of my father's hired servants have more than enough bread, but I perish here with hunger! I will arise and go to my father, and I will say to him, "Father, I have sinned against heaven and before you. I am no longer worthy to be called your son. Treat me as one of your hired servants."' And he arose and came to his father. But while he was still a long way off, his father saw him and felt compassion, and ran and embraced him and kissed him. And the son said to him, 'Father, I have sinned against heaven and before you. I am no longer worthy to be called your son.' But the father said to his servants, 'Bring quickly the best robe, and put it on him, and put a ring on his hand, and shoes on his feet. And bring the fattened calf and kill it, and let us eat and celebrate. For this my son was dead, and is alive again; he was lost, and is found.' And they began to celebrate.

"Now his older son was in the field, and as he came
and drew near to the house, he heard music and danc-
ing. And he called one of the servants and asked what
these things meant. And he said to him, 'Your brother
has come, and your father has killed the fattened calf,
because he has received him back safe and sound.' But
he was angry and refused to go in. His father came out
and entreated him, but he answered his father, 'Look,
these many years I have served you, and I never disobeyed your command, yet you never gave me a young
goat, that I might celebrate with my friends. But when
this son of yours came, who has devoured your property
with prostitutes, you killed the fattened calf for him!'
And he said to him, 'Son, you are always with me, and
all that is mine is yours. It was fitting to celebrate and be
glad, for this your brother was dead, and is alive; he was
lost, and is found.'"

The context for this chapter is provided in verses 1 and 2. In
verse 1 we're told "the tax collectors and sinners were all drawing
near to hear him." What an amazing sentence! What an amazing
circumstance! Since Adam and Eve in the Garden, men in their
sin have sewn fig leaves and hidden themselves from God. But
here, they come close to him. They want to hear him. This might
surprise us if we keep in mind a passage like Isaiah 53, where
we're told:

> He had no beauty or majesty to attract us to him,
> nothing in his appearance that we should desire him.
> He was despised and rejected by mankind. . . .
> he was despised, and we held him in low esteem.
> (vv. 2–3 NIV)

Nevertheless Jesus draws sinners to hear him.

But Luke 15 alerts us to a conflict. Verse 2: "The Pharisees and the scribes grumbled, saying, 'This man receives sinners and eats with them.'" What the Pharisees think they see disturbs them. All they see are sinners. And all they can think of is how unclean these sinners are, and how inappropriate it is that a rabbi, a holy man, should dirty himself with their presence. They say, "This man receives sinners . . ." and that's *bad* news to them. They utter the most precious words imaginable—Jesus receives sinners—not to commend Jesus but to condemn Jesus along with sinners.

The Pharisees don't see the truly beautiful spiritual realities behind "tax collectors and sinners . . . all drawing near to hear" Jesus (v. 1). In reply, Jesus tells three parables that make one over-arching point: heaven rejoices over every repentant sinner. In the first two parables we get the statement of the main point. In the third parable we get an illustration of the point. These three vivid stories are designed to open the blinded eyes of the Pharisees. This one main point provides, I pray, motivation in evangelism to emphasize the necessity and beauty of repentance.

Heaven Rejoices Over Every Repentant Sinner

We see that heaven rejoices over every repentant sinner in each of the three parables. The parables are parallel, teaching much the same thing with slight differences in emphasis. But notice first the punch line for each parable:

- Verse 7: "Just so, I tell you, there will be more joy in heaven over one sinner who repents than over ninety-nine righteous persons who need no repentance."
- Verse 10: "Just so, I tell you, there is joy before the angels of God over one sinner who repents."

- Verses 22–23: "The father said to his servants, 'Bring quickly the best robe, and put it on him, and put a ring on his hand, and shoes on his feet. And bring the fattened calf and kill it, and let us eat and celebrate.'"

This picture of rejoicing is what the Pharisees missed, and what we perhaps seldom consider. Repentance brings happiness to heaven. Repentance isn't merely a duty that men perform. Repentance isn't merely the "hard part," the unpleasant conversation that saints must have with sinners in evangelism. No! Repentance is one fountain of joy in heaven! Nothing prompts a party in heaven like the turning of a soul from sin to the Savior!

And there's a disproportion here. Think of verse 7 again. Ninety-nine righteous people cannot produce more happiness in heaven than just one sinner who turns from their sin toward God! Angels sing and celebrate over a single soul who repents.

And what of this rejoicing? This joy in heaven—what is it? And what is it like?

Heaven's joy is not a fleeting, temporary, misty joy. All rejoicing on this side of glory is temporary and marked by decay. Our longest periods of happiness seem so short-lived. Soon circumstances change and our happiness is dashed. Before long our hearts cool and our memories fade and along with them goes our joy. We now lack the ability to perpetually enjoy ourselves on this side of glory.

Our hearts fail to exult in God even when something as miraculous and glorious as repentance unto eternal life happens. I know this in my own life. I sometimes remember a person's repentance unto faith and am moved. Sometimes. But I mourn in shame that those remembrances are so infrequent and quickly passing. My heart is sometimes unmoved even at the remembrance of God's sovereign work in my own repentance!

But heaven's happiness is not like our fleeting happiness in this life. The joy of heaven is constant, full, permanent, and solid. This means the rejoicing in heaven over a sinner's repentance never goes away or fades.

It's a joy that expands in *quality*. It is everlasting, never diminishing, always wonder-filled rejoicing. This joy grows richer, deeper, stronger, more satisfying, fulfilling, agreeable, blessed, delightful, good, gratifying, pleasing, exhilarating, elating, and enlivening for all eternity.

And it is a joy that expands in *quantity* as well. Verse 6 again: "And when he comes home, he calls together his friends and his neighbors, saying to them, 'Rejoice with me, for I have found my sheep that was lost.'" And verse 9: "And when she has found it, she calls together her friends and neighbors, saying, 'Rejoice with me, for I have found the coin that I had lost.'" And then verse 23: the father says to his servants, "let us eat and celebrate." The chorus of celebrants grows as each individual sinner is brought safely home in repentance. Friends, neighbors, and angels are called together to share the joy.

Who are these friends and neighbors? It must be us—the Christian, the evangelist. We are not only the *means* of bringing heaven joy through evangelism, but also the *invited guests* who share in that joy! When we do the work of evangelism and call people to repentance, we store up our own eternal joy. For we will forever partake in this celebration. Our God will one day call us into the halls of his banquet and bid us delight in the miracle of those once-lost, now-found repentant sinners brought home on the shoulders of Christ Jesus through evangelism. *If heaven is happy at the repentance of sinners, evangelists will share in that happiness for preaching repentance to sinners.* We will experience this rejoicing for all the unending days of glory!

Heaven rejoices over every repentant sinner. Do we anticipate sharing in that rejoicing when, in evangelism, it comes to explaining repentance?

Seven Reasons Repentance Is Particularly Beautiful to Heaven

But we might ask ourselves, what is it about repentance that makes it so beautiful to heaven? What does God see in the nature of repentance that Pharisees and some evangelists miss?

These three parables show us seven reasons heaven rejoices over sinners who repent, and these seven reasons should motivate us in evangelism.

1. Because the repentance of the sinner is the goal of the gospel

In the parable of the lost sheep and the lost coin, Jesus puts the hearers in the story. "What man of you" (v. 4) and "Or what woman" (v. 8) includes every man or woman. In choosing a story with which everyone could easily identify, Jesus also puts his hearers in the point of view of heaven. That's what the Pharisees were missing— heaven's point of view. Here's what they are meant to see standing in the shoes of the imaginary shepherd and woman: God making a sacrificial and diligent search for the lost and reaching his goal.

See the sacrifice in verse 4? The shepherd "leaves the ninety-nine in open country" to "go after the one that is lost, until he finds it." Some commentators suggest the ninety-nine were in a place of safety, so the shepherd could afford to leave them for the one. But the text doesn't say that. It says the flock was in "open country." They were vulnerable to attack, to wandering, to the elements. The point is not that the ninety-nine were safe, leaving the shepherd unencumbered to find one. The point is the shepherd loves the one with such love that he's willing to take great risks to secure the one lost sheep. He would do that for any single sheep appointed to his fold.

Moreover, God's search for the lost is diligent. That is pictured in the woman's search for the lost coin. Verse 8 again: "Or what woman, having ten silver coins, if she loses one coin, does not light a lamp and sweep the house and seek diligently until she finds it?" That coin was a drachma, about one day's wages. One day's earnings out of ten is no small portion. How many of us have had a wallet full of cash and realized we misplaced a $5 bill? And though we have nearly all our cash, we look frantically for that $5, don't we? So see the woman's diligence: She lights a lamp. She sweeps the house. She seeks—*diligently.*

The result is that the shepherd and the woman find what they seek: the lost coin and the lost sheep. Repentance is another word for heaven's finding lost people.

Don't miss this: these two parables present repentance as the accomplished work of the One who searches. Repentance is God's work in the sinner. The New Hampshire Confession of Faith captures this well: "We believe that Repentance and Faith are sacred duties, *and also inseparable graces, wrought in our souls by the regenerating Spirit of God.*"

So does the Canons of Dordt. Article 10, entitled, "Conversion as the Work of God," reads,

> . . . *conversion must not be credited to man,* as though one distinguishes himself by free choice from others who are furnished with equal or sufficient grace for faith and conversion (as the proud heresy of Pelagius maintains). No, [*conversion*] *must be credited to God:* just as from eternity he chose his own in Christ, so within time he effectively calls them, *grants them faith and repentance,* and, having

rescued them from the dominion of darkness, brings
them into the kingdom of his Son. . . .

The mission of our Lord is a diligent search and rescue of lost
people. Jesus remarks a few chapters after our chapter, "The Son of
Man came to seek and to save the lost" (Luke 19:10). Evangelism
is but the continuance of that mission to seek and save. Each
time the evangelist succeeds and a sinner repents, heaven rejoices
because heaven's mission is accomplished in miniature.

2. Because the unrepentant sinner is of great worth in heaven's sight

Heaven rejoices because the unrepentant sinner is of great
worth in heaven's sight.

Why doesn't God relax and settle for the great numbers he
already has in his possession? Why doesn't he look at the ninety-
nine and feel satisfied? Why doesn't he clutch the nine coins and
shrug off the one? Why carry out such a diligent search?

Is it not because God places such high value on the soul that
belongs to him? These are sheep and coins with *owners*. This one
wandering lamb belongs to a shepherd. This one missing coin
belongs to a woman. They are owned, so they are *valued*.

There is a poverty that comes to their owner when they are
missing. There is a wanting in the owner's heart. The owner feels
their absence. That is why he cannot remain with the ninety-nine
but feels compelled to go after the solitary sheep. That is why she
cannot sit comfortably in the house but must ransack it until she
has the coin. Each feels the loss. So when the sheep and coin are
found, the owner feels their value once again. There is a satisfac-
tion in possessing them again. Their value and worth are realized
in the owner's sight.

So consider verse 5: "When he has found [the lost sheep], he
lays it on his shoulders, rejoicing." He places the sheep in a place

of safety. In his happiness, after perhaps a long and wearisome search, strength returns to his body and every burden is light. So it is when Christ finds the lost sheep through repentance. "He tends his flock like a shepherd: He gathers the lambs in his arms and carries them close to his heart" (Isa. 40:11 NIV).

When the unrepentant is found by the Owner of their souls, their worth and value are once again felt and realized by God. Heaven rejoices over every repentant sinner—because the sinner is of great worth to God.

3. Because life apart from God is so devastatingly ugly (vv. 12–16)

Heaven also rejoices because life apart from God is so devastatingly ugly. In other words, the beauty of repentance is seen most clearly against the backdrop of sin. Consider the younger son's steady decline into squalor in verses 12–16.

> "And the younger of them said to his father, 'Father, give me the share of property that is coming to me.' And he divided his property between them. Not many days later, the younger son gathered all he had and took a journey into a far country, and there he squandered his property in reckless living. And when he had spent everything, a severe famine arose in that country, and he began to be in need. So he went and hired himself out to one of the citizens of that country, who sent him into his fields to feed the pigs. And he was longing to be fed with the pods that pigs ate, and no one gave him anything."

The son starts with everything. But he's ungrateful and impatient, so he makes himself *fatherless* (v. 12). Because he wants to gratify his sinful desires, he also makes himself *homeless* in "a far country" (v. 13). Without self-control or delayed gratification, he ends up *penniless* (v. 14). In the end he is *friendless and foodless* (vv. 15–16).

Right about that time he's singing a little Billie Holiday: "When you've got money, you've got lots of friends. They come crowdin' around your door. When the money's gone and spending ends, they don't come 'round no more." His life slides deep into squalor and loneliness. If you live for yourself you'll soon live by yourself.

This is what our lives look like from the vantage point of heaven. God the Father watches his rich but rebellious children squander his love and his riches as they run from him.

So it is with sinners and God the Father. Sinners want all the wealth of creation and all the "freedom" of life apart from God. They do not want God himself. They do not understand his fatherhood. They refuse to requite his love. Unless God restrains them, they squander their lives and waste away as they chase every desire.

Against this backdrop, repentance is beautiful! Repentance appears as the good life that it truly is. The saltiness of sin gives way to the sweetness of sanctification. "Life" apart from God is really a slow death. Apart from God we are living to die. But repentance is dying to live. It is dying to self to find life in Christ. That's why repentance is so beautiful to heaven's sight and causes such rejoicing.

4. Because repentance begins to value God properly (vv. 17–20)

Repentance appears so beautiful to heaven because it begins to value God properly. Notice what happens to the son in verses 17–20.

First comes a *recognition*. Verse 17: "But when he came to himself, he said, 'How many of my father's hired servants have more than enough bread, but I perish here with hunger!'" Repentance recognizes the goodness of God. The son was a servant in fields begging for the pods that swine eat. But in his father's house, the hired servants have more than enough bread! Unlike the master in the far country, the younger son's father is generous toward those who serve him. In turning, the son begins to recognize something about the goodness of his father.

Second, comes a *resolution*. Verse 18: "I will arise and go to my father, and I will say to him, 'Father, I have sinned against heaven and before you.'" The son decides his place is with his father. And more than that, he decides to make one of the greatest confessions in the Bible. He confesses that He has sinned against heaven (God) as well as his father. One commentator observes, "He was aware of a holy God and a broken Law."[13] And another: "He confesses without conditions and without qualifications. He makes no excuses. He offers no explanations. He had sinned. Period. The problem with most confessions is that they primarily express regret for the consequences of sin rather than regret for sin itself."[14]

Third, there comes a *resignation*. Verse 19: "I am no longer worthy to be called your son. Treat me as one of your hired servants." He sees himself and his sins in light of God's goodness and greatness. Knowing his depravity, he resigns any thoughts of sonship. He would settle to be a servant in his father's house. He can't claim to be a son given his sin. He can only hope to serve. Consider what Charles Spurgeon said about this:

> The prodigal, when he said, "I will arise and go to my father," became in a measure reformed from that very moment. How, say you? Why, he left the swine-trough: more, he left the wine cup, and he left the harlots. He did not go with the harlot on his arm, and the wine cup in his hand, and say, "I will take these with me, and go to my father." It could not be. These were all left, and

though he had not goodness to bring, yet he did not try
to keep his sins and come to Christ.[15]

So it is with true repentance. The men and women who turn
to God begin to see God as they never have before. They begin
to recognize the greatness of God's love. They begin to see his
generous character. They understand the holiness of God and the
wretchedness of sin. They're brought low. They're humbled. They
know God is generous so they come to him. But they know their
sins are great, so they make no demands on God. The humility of
repentance does not set its gaze on much, just the hope of inclu-
sion. The repentant person pleads only for a servant's place.

In all of this the praiseworthy character of God is shown.
Repentance is beautiful because it finds God beautiful, just as this
young son now sees his own father as wonderful.

5. Because repentance is the occasion for the display of the riches of God's grace (vv. 22–23)

Sure enough, the son returns to the father and makes his
confession in verse 21. No doubt he is filthy and ragged. He was
once finely manicured, a prince at the party. But now he returns a
pauper, thinking himself orphaned by his sin. He has no claim to
sonship and does not expect to be treated as one.

But his repentance creates a theater for the display of God's
rich grace. See how the father responds to the lost son. Verse 20:
"He arose and came to his father. But while he was still a long way
off, his father saw him and felt compassion, and ran and embraced
him and kissed him." And verses 22–23: "But the father said to his
servants, 'Bring quickly the best robe, and put it on him, and put a
ring on his hand, and shoes on his feet. And bring the fattened calf
and kill it, and let *us eat and celebrate*'" (emphasis added).

See the excellent qualities that shine forth from the father.
There is compassion. There is tenderness in his embrace and his

kisses. There is adoption and generosity. The father receives his son *as a son*. He places a robe and ring on him, signs of his sonship. And there is that joy again—kill the fattened calf and let's celebrate!

Here's where the gospel defies all human expectation. We think the son might be chastised. We think the father would have been generous to allow the son back as a servant. We think the son could and perhaps should have been cut off. He has spent his inheritance. How can he come back asking for anything?

But the father in the story, a pale reflection of God the Father, pours out the storehouses of his grace and mercy at the far away sign of his son's repentance! The far-away sighting of a sinner's return elicits the fountain of God's love! The sinner who turns finds that he turns right into the waiting arms of his God. God receives the penitent with the riches of heaven—the robes of Christ, the signet of sonship, the banquet of salvation! A kingdom for a beggar—that's what heaven is! And it makes the riches of God's grace all the more glorious.

As evangelists, we get to call people back into the rich, merciful arms of the Father. Calling people to repentance isn't a rude intrusion in their lives. It is an indescribable invitation to the tenderness and compassion of the Father.

6. Because repentance reflects the miracle of the new birth (v. 24)

Verse 24 reads, "For this my son was dead, and is alive again; he was lost, and is found." Repentance causes heaven to rejoice because it reflects and is a fruit of the new birth. When we see a repentant man, we know a resurrection has happened. The one who was dead in trespasses and sins in which he once walked has been made alive again through Christ!

The lostness wasn't just a misplacement. It was a death. The son had been dead to the father. But in the miracle of repentance he has been raised to newness of life. He has been brought back— not as a corpse for a funeral—but as a living soul for a banquet. Heaven finds repentance beautiful because it brings back to life those that sin had killed.

7. Because the sinner's repentance exposes the hardness of the self-righteous (vv. 25–30)

There's one final reason heaven finds repentance beautiful. It's because the repentance of one sinner exposes the unrepentance and self-righteousness of others. That's what we see in verses 25–30.

The second son, the older brother, comes into the picture. He hears the party (v. 25) and seeks an answer (v. 26). When he hears the brother has returned and the fattened calf killed because his brother is "safe and sound," he loses it. Verse 28: "But he was angry and refused to go in."

Though his father entreats him gently, all the older son can see is his own righteousness. Leon Morris observes, "The proud and self-righteous always feel that they are not treated as well as they deserve."[16] So he makes his case with his father. Verses 29–30: "Look, these many years I have served you [literally, slaved for you], and I never disobeyed your command, yet you never gave me a young goat, that I might celebrate with my friends. But when this son of yours came, who has devoured your property with prostitutes, you killed the fattened calf for him!"

How many of us have a difficult time detecting the fault in the older son's thinking? How many of us sympathize with him? The Pharisees certainly did. In fact, Leon Morris writes, "We can easily imagine the elder brother saying of his father, 'This man receives sinners and eats with them.'"[17]

The father's response shows the son's heart. The elder son did not know what he had: "He said to him, 'Son, you are always with me, and all that is mine is yours'" (v. 31). Again, to quote Leon Morris: "He did not really understand what being a son means. That is perhaps why he didn't understand what being a father means. He could not see why his father should be so full of joy at the return of the prodigal."[18] He could not see that celebration is necessary. The father says in verse 32, "It was fitting [or necessary] to celebrate and be glad, for this your brother was dead, and is alive; he was lost, and is found."

The sinner's repentance exposes the hardness of the self-righteous. A sinner's repentance should be good for a saint's heart. Though we like to imagine ourselves to be the younger brother, many of us are actually the older brother. In our self-righteousness, we tend to think that self-help is how we made it. We tend to think those broken by sin ought to mend themselves and their ways. Then they become to us the "deserving spiritual poor." Then, maybe—just maybe—we will celebrate at their repentance.

But in God's sight, the first sign of repentance requires a celebration by the godly. Repentance is for the joy of the church. It is for our revival and celebration.

Applications

There are five things I am now fighting to remember as an evangelist, based on studying Luke 15. These things encourage me to emphasize repentance when sharing the gospel rather than to shrink back.

1. ***Remember that repentance is for the joy of heaven, the joy of the church, and the joy of the sinner.*** When we call a man to repent, we call him to his joy. We need

never be embarrassed about calling people to an eternal joy that satisfies every party concerned.

2. *Remember that calling a person to repent of sin is calling the person to recognize his or her worth in God's sight.* Sin has been destroying a person's dignity and value as a being made in the image of God. It is repentance that restores that value.

3. *Remember that what we are calling people to in repentance isn't merely to give up this life's pleasures; it is to gain heaven's greater pleasures.* In the presence of the Lord is pleasure forevermore. Repentance returns a lost man to the presence and pleasures of the Lord.

4. *Remember that our emphasis on repentance isn't so much an emphasis on do's and don'ts in the Christian life. It is more fundamentally an emphasis on seeing life as it really is—including God.* Christianity and moralism are two different religions. While the Christian subscribes to high morality, his morality is not what makes him a Christian. It's his unique covenant relationship with God wherein he comes to enjoy God forever that makes him a Christian. Repentance opens his eyes to see and savor God.

5. *Remember when we call a person to repent, we're calling him or her into what God finds beautiful.*

CHAPTER 5

The Certainty of God's Victory
(Isaiah 36—37)

Mark Dever

Things look bad right now.

The evil and bitter nature of sin presses us on every side. We contend with our own sin. Problems in our churches occupy us, such as false teachers who go unopposed. Movies and television hold up evangelical, biblical teaching for mockery and ridicule. The press portrays Christians as silly or, worse, as hostile and menacing. Our federal courts campaigned for a decade to legalize same-sex marriage, resulting in the recent Supreme Court decision on the matter. And corporate America forces out CEOs who believe what the president himself said he believed only a few years ago (but no longer does)—that marriage is between a man and a woman. That was hardly a controversial statement for most of our lives. The speed of the change is breathtaking. So-called toleration seems to be a one-way street. Divergent opinions are by definition intolerant. The Christian life is increasingly the "alternative lifestyle."

Elsewhere in the world, Christians face intense violence. Christians face their worst persecution in Egypt in seven hundred years. Though Christians in Egypt comprise the largest Christian minority in the Middle East—around 10 percent of the population—many Muslim citizens are literally trying to drive them out of the country. Last August, over forty church buildings were destroyed on one day over a few hours.

In Nigeria, Christians are killed, and their families are threatened with death if they bury the bodies. The killers want the bodies left unburied as a warning to anyone who would follow Christ.

In Afghanistan, Christianity is outlawed, and the conversion of Muslims is a crime. The Taliban regularly attempts to kill people suspected of being Christians. These tragedies go on day by day. And we're not even talking about trying to reach the millions who've never heard the gospel of Christ in Eritrea, or Pakistan, or Iran.

Does it not therefore seem a little far-fetched to devote chapters and books, conferences and sermons, to the topic of evangelism? Perhaps we should instead tar the ark, repair the walls, and call our lawyers!

Before we sink into cynicism or despair, though, it is worth recalling what Paul told the Ephesian church: "Our struggle is not against flesh and blood, but against the rulers, against the authorities, against the powers of this dark world and against the spiritual forces of evil in the heavenly realms" (Eph. 6:12).[19] Might our struggles not point toward a larger drama, and a drama which itself points toward reasons for hope?

Hope is the confidence that something good will happen in the future. The Bible teaches that both God and the devil work to destroy our hopes, the devil so that we stop hoping altogether, God so that we stop hoping in the passing things of this world. To draw us into the larger hope for which we were made, God lovingly peels these smaller hopes from our grip. He has a long record of placing his people into situations where human hope exhausts itself. Think of Joseph in prison, or the children of Israel with the Red Sea in front of them and the Egyptian army behind them. Think of David before Goliath, or Jonah in the fish. Most of all, think of Jesus in the Garden of Gethsemane, and then dying on a cross.

The topic of evangelism may cause fear and discouragement in the hearts of many ministers. We may feel ill-equipped or defeated personally. And we face a world that feels more hateful to the gospel than it did in 2006 when the Together for the Gospel conferences began. But could it be that God means through all of these things to dash our smaller hopes so that we put our hope in this larger thing—*that if he is with us, we cannot fail?*

Our churches must learn this lesson for the sake of evangelism. And it's the lesson of the story at the heart of Isaiah's book in chapters 36 and 37. If God is with us, we cannot fail.

In these chapters, we find the "great public event" of Isaiah's lifetime, the event that defined an era just as the Civil War defined the nineteenth century for anyone living in the United States. This great public event was the Assyrian assault on Jerusalem and its dramatic conclusion.

Isaiah's own ministry could be characterized as forty years spent preparing people for this event, followed by ten years of unpacking what happened, just as Moses' ministry was spent preparing a people for another great public event in Israel's life, followed by years of explaining it. And the basic lesson of Isaiah's ministry? God's judgment and salvation would come through trusting in God alone.

As we read and meditate on ten different scenes from these chapters, I pray that you will trust the Lord alone for your salvation, for your ministry, and even for your evangelism.

Scene #1: The Assyrian Invasion

Chapter 36 begins, "In the fourteenth year of King Hezekiah's reign, Sennacherib king of Assyria attacked all the fortified cities of Judah and captured them."

The verse places us in 701 BC in the southern kingdom of Judah. But let's back up and recall the larger history. Four decades earlier, in 745 BC, the Assyrians had taken Damascus and subjugated Aram (or Syria). That opened the way for them to move south into Palestine. Just two years later, in 743, the northern kingdom of Israel began to pay protection or tribute to the Assyrian king (2 Kings 15:19). In 727 the Assyrian king died, and Israel stopped paying tribute. God decided to use this moment to judge Israel for centuries of idolatry. So, in 724, Assyria invaded Israel. They laid siege to the capitol city of Samaria for two years, and finally took it in 722 BC.

The Assyrian Empire had a policy of relocating conquered peoples far from their native lands in order to dilute their national identity and to cut people off from the power of their local gods (see 2 Kings 17). By Assyria's own records, they deported 27,290 Israelite citizens to other parts of the empire following the 722 conquest. They decapitated the society and subjugated any survivors. To top it all off, they brought in people from Babylon and resettled them in Israel (2 Kings 17:24). In short, the northern kingdom was destroyed.

Meanwhile, down south, Isaiah's ministry began around 740 BC with the death of King Uzziah, who had reigned fifty-two years. His son Jotham briefly followed him, followed in turn by his own son Ahaz, who reigned for sixteen years. In 735 BC, Ahaz put the nation of Judah into vassalage to Assyria and its gods in order to save Judah from invasion by the northern kingdom of Israel and Syria (2 Kings 16:7–9). Ahaz also offered human sacrifices to Baal. During these years, Judah was in decline, losing portions of its land to the Philistines, the Edomites, and the Syrians.

Ahaz eventually died. His son Hezekiah succeeded him on the throne. Isaiah convinced King Hezekiah to stop paying the Assyrians tribute (see 2 Kings 18:7). And now the worst fears of Judah were realized. Assyria, after putting down a rebellion in Babylon, turned its full attention to Palestine. The Assyrians crushed the Philistines, conquered Tyre, and defeated the Egyptians. Then they invaded Judah with tens of thousands of troops. And they were successful. So says Isaiah 36:1: "Sennacherib king of Assyria attacked all the fortified cities of Judah and captured them." The people of Judah were beyond human help.

The Assyrians weren't merely conquerors and empire-builders like the Egyptians or the Greeks. Instead, they were renowned for their brutality. They would torture their enemies and cut them into pieces. They would burn people alive in order to terrorize the population. They would sometimes skin the defeated rulers and display their skins on the walls of the conquered city. They impaled prisoners on stakes. They decapitated many. All of these things are shown in their own carved records. They liked to brag! But those records never show a dead Assyrian. They presented themselves as indestructible.

How then were the people of Jerusalem feeling when Sennacherib attacked Judah? Like God had let them down?

The nation had undergone a great reformation under Hezekiah. Hezekiah had refurbished the Temple, reconsecrated the priests, reinstituted the Passover celebration, and invited the survivors from the northern tribes to join them. The Bible says:

> There was great joy in Jerusalem, for since the days of
> Solomon son of David king of Israel there had been noth-
> ing like this in Jerusalem. . . . When all this had ended,
> the Israelites who were there went out to the towns of
> Judah, smashed the sacred stones and cut down the
> Asherah poles. They destroyed the high places and the
> altars throughout Judah. . . . (2 Chron. 30:26; 31:1)

If they had been so faithful, why was God letting this terrible
thing happen now? Isaiah had been exhorting them for decades to
trust in God alone. Had they been foolish to do so?

There is a lesson here about our *fears*: In a fallen world, our
fears don't always lie to us. Some fears come true. Repentance
doesn't get us out of all of our trials. That church board may reject
your ideas about evangelism. That friend may not speak to you
again after you witness to him. Remember 1 John 3:13: "Do not
be surprised, my brothers, if the world hates you." Do you fear the
world hating you? It just might. Some of our fears do come true.

But our fears always lie to us about how important they are.

Scene #2: The Field Commander's Speech

Do Jerusalem's fears come true? The Assyrian field commander's speech in the next scene tempts us to believe they do.

> Then the king of Assyria sent his field commander
> with a large army from Lachish to King Hezekiah at
> Jerusalem. When the commander stopped at the aque-
> duct of the Upper Pool, on the road to the Washerman's
> Field, Eliakim son of Hilkiah the palace administrator,
> Shebna the secretary, and Joah son of Asaph the recorder
> went out to him. The field commander said to them,
> "Tell Hezekiah, 'This is what the great king, the king of

Assyria, says: On what are you basing this confidence of
yours? You say you have strategy and military strength—
but you speak only empty words. On whom are you
depending, that you rebel against me? Look now, you
are depending on Egypt, that splintered reed of a staff,
which pierces a man's hand and wounds him if he leans
on it! Such is Pharaoh king of Egypt to all who depend
on him. And if you say to me, "We are depending on the
LORD our God"—isn't he the one whose high places and
altars Hezekiah removed, saying to Judah and Jerusalem,
"You must worship before this altar"? Come now, make
a bargain with my master, the king of Assyria: I will
give you two thousand horses—if you can put riders on
them! How then can you repulse one officer of the least
of my master's officials, even though you are depending
on Egypt for chariots and horsemen? Furthermore, have
I come to attack and destroy this land without the LORD?
The LORD himself told me to march against this country
and destroy it.'" Then Eliakim, Shebna and Joah said to
the field commander, "Please speak to your servants in
Aramaic, since we understand it. Don't speak to us in
Hebrew in the hearing of the people on the wall." But
the commander replied, "Was it only to your master and
you that my master sent me to say these things, and not
to the men sitting on the wall—who, like you, will have
to eat their own filth and drink their own urine?" Then
the commander stood and called out in Hebrew, "Hear
the words of the great king, the king of Assyria! This is
what the king says: Do not let Hezekiah deceive you. He
cannot deliver you! Do not let Hezekiah persuade you to
trust in the LORD when he says, 'The LORD will surely
deliver us; this city will not be given into the hand of the

king of Assyria.' 'Do not listen to Hezekiah. This is what
the king of Assyria says: Make peace with me and come
out to me. Then every one of you will eat from his own
vine and fig tree and drink water from his own cistern,
until I come and take you to a land like your own—a
land of grain and new wine, a land of bread and vineyards. Do not let Hezekiah mislead you when he says,
'The Lord will deliver us.' Has the god of any nation ever
delivered his land from the hand of the king of Assyria?
Where are the gods of Hamath and Arpad? Where are
the gods of Sepharvaim? Have they rescued Samaria
from my hand? Who of all the gods of these countries
has been able to save his land from me? How then can
the Lord deliver Jerusalem from my hand?" But the
people remained silent and said nothing in reply, because
the king had commanded, "Do not answer him." (Isa.
36:2–21)

Lachish, mentioned in verse 2, was the second largest city in
Judah, and capturing it was essential for isolating and capturing
Jerusalem. Today in London's British Museum you can view the
relief sculpture from Sennacherib's palace in Nineveh that shows
this very siege and capture of Lachish.

The biblical passage begins with envoys from Hezekiah meeting Sennacherib's field commander in the same place that the
Lord had told Hezekiah's father Ahaz to stand firm in his faith
(Isa. 7:3). But now the Assyrian asks the question that drives the
whole story: What are you basing your confidence on? It's like God
himself was speaking to them again through this commander,
pressing on them the question that drove Isaiah's whole ministry.
The field commander asks again in verse 5, "On whom are you
depending?"

The commander calls their bluff should they point to Egypt as their trust. Yet then he oversteps and reveals that he misunderstands Hezekiah's reformation. He was a diplomat who knew facts, but not their significance and meaning. Yes, altars to Baal and other false gods had been torn down, but that wasn't an attack on religion, as it would have been in Assyria. The reformation promoted devotion to the true God, the Holy One of Israel.

Still, this Assyrian officer knew how to exploit the fears of his audience. He addressed his unsettling words to Hezekiah's envoys within earshot of the soldiers at the gate. In Hebrew! And what satanic stuff we find in verses 15 and 18. He calls them foolish for being tempted to trust in God. Then in verses 19 and 20 he puts God into the category of false gods and denies that he can deliver Jerusalem from the Assyrians. Truth and error are mixed together. It was true that Egypt was unreliable. It was true that Hezekiah had destroyed many altars, and that the Assyrians had conquered many nations. But these truths are placed in service of the lie that God would abandon his people. God will never abandon his people. To abandon his people—to abandon us—is to abandon his own promises. And he will never be untrue to his own Word.

Here is a lesson for us about *trust*: the most important thing about us is the object of our trust. "In whom will you trust?" (v. 5). The field commander's speech demonstrates how utterly helpless the people were. Yet their helplessness was the doorway to complete trust in God.

So it is with us. As Paul says to the Corinthians, "when I am weak, then I am strong" (2 Cor. 12:10). And understanding this reality should help our churches in the evangelistic task. There is no such thing as a pastor too discouraged to be re-invigorated by the Lord; nor a church too cold to be changed by God's Word; nor a people too hostile to be converted by God's Spirit when we preach the gospel!

Scene #3: Hezekiah Hears the
Assyrian Ultimatum

How then will Hezekiah respond to the field commander's speech? This brings us to scene 3, in which the envoys report the Assyrian ultimatum to Hezekiah:

> Then Eliakim son of Hilkiah the palace administrator,
> Shebna the secretary, and Joah son of Asaph the recorder
> went to Hezekiah, with their clothes torn, and told him
> what the field commander had said.
>   When King Hezekiah heard this, he tore his clothes
> and put on sackcloth and went into the temple of the
> LORD. (Isa. 36:22—37:1)

In the ancient Near East, tearing the clothes was a sign of distress and mourning. So Hezekiah demonstrates his distress, but then immediately turns to God for help by going to the temple. He could have turned to Egypt, or idols, or his own military strength, as kings of Judah had done before. Or he could have sunk into despair. Instead, he goes to the one true God.

Brother pastor, when you're in a time of increasing hopelessness, where do you go? To whom do you turn? Here's a lesson about *making choices*: choose to go to God with your problems.

But that's not all that Hezekiah does!

Scene #4: Hezekiah Asks Isaiah
to Pray for the Remnant

He also asks Isaiah to pray for Israel, which brings us to scene 4.

> [Hezekiah] sent Eliakim the palace administrator,
> Shebna the secretary, and the leading priests, all wearing

sackcloth, to the prophet Isaiah son of Amoz. They told
him, "This is what Hezekiah says: This day is a day of
distress and rebuke and disgrace, as when children come
to the point of birth and there is no strength to deliver
them. It may be that the LORD your God will hear the
words of the field commander, whom his master, the king
of Assyria, has sent to ridicule the living God, and that
he will rebuke him for the words the LORD your God has
heard. Therefore pray for the remnant that still survives."
(Isa. 37:2–4)

Hezekiah clearly understands that the Lord is the object of
the Assyrian mockery. So Hezekiah prays, and he calls on Isaiah
to pray.

What a simple but profound lesson for us on *prayer*: when you
are in trouble, turn to God in his Word and prayer.

Jesus taught his disciples that they "should always pray and not
give up" (Luke 18:1). That applies to you even while reading this
chapter. Prayer is what faith looks like. We talk to God because
we believe what he's told us in his Word—that he *wants* to help us,
that he *can* help us, that he *will* help us, if we ask him to. Through
prayer and God's Word, God draws us into his own purposes.

Of course, prayer is powerful not because of who is praying.
In our text, it's a repenting and desperate king who prays. Prayer is
powerful because of who is prayed to—the sovereign God of the
whole world; the God of Abraham, Isaac, and Jacob; the Holy One
of Israel! It's the same with us. We bring honor to God by believing his promises, and by boldly approaching the throne of grace.
Prayers of intercession are in fact prayers of praise. By our asking
we testify to God's faithfulness and reliability.

Dear church leaders and elders, if there is to be any culture
of evangelism in our churches, it will begin in our prayers. I am

so thankful for the time that our congregation in Washington has to pray together—in our morning and evening services, in our elders meeting and in our families, in small groups, and in our own personal times with the Lord. We pray for ourselves. We pray for unreached peoples, persecuted Christians, the advance of the gospel, other evangelical churches in our city by name, and many other things. God's grace has made us a praying church. Prayer is the preview of God's action.

Scene #5: Isaiah Delivers God's Word to Hezekiah

Wonderfully, God answers Hezekiah's prayers:

> When King Hezekiah's officials came to Isaiah, Isaiah said to them, "Tell your master, 'This is what the LORD says: Do not be afraid of what you have heard—those words with which the underlings of the king of Assyria have blasphemed me. Listen! I am going to put a spirit in him so that when he hears a certain report, he will return to his own country, and there I will have him cut down with the sword.'" (Isa. 37:5–7)

I love the dismissive reference to "underlings" (or young men). Neither the Lord nor his prophet is intimidated by the mightiest of men. They are but dust! God condemns the field commander's speech as blasphemy. And then he reveals his plan: he will destroy the Assyrian king.

Do you see the lesson here about God's *promises*? God promises to save his people. And he promises to destroy those who would destroy them.

In our churches, we hold out God's promises to one another. We do this when preaching God's Word. We do this when singing and celebrating baptisms and the Lord's Supper. We encourage each other to persevere by reminding each other of the fellowship that we will experience with our Savior when he returns. We are a people shaped by God's promises, like iron shavings pulled along by a magnet. His promises are the magnet that gives us direction. And God promises to save his people!

Scene #6: Sennacherib's Word to Hezekiah

What will happen with Jerusalem and Hezekiah? Will Isaiah's words get back to Sennacherib and cause him to retreat in fear?

> When the field commander heard that the king of Assyria had left Lachish, he withdrew and found the king fighting against Libnah. Now Sennacherib received a report that Tirhakah, the Cushite king [of Egypt], was marching out to fight against him. When he heard it, he sent messengers to Hezekiah with this word: "Say to Hezekiah king of Judah: Do not let the God you depend on deceive you when he says, 'Jerusalem will not be handed over to the king of Assyria.' Surely you have heard what the kings of Assyria have done to all the countries, destroying them completely. And will you be delivered? Did the gods of the nations that were destroyed by my forefathers deliver them—the gods of Gozan, Haran, Rezeph and the people of Eden who were in Tel Assar? Where is the king of Hamath, the king of Arpad, the king of the city of Sepharvaim, or of Hena or Ivvah?" (Isa. 37:8–13)

It seems that Sennacherib had now moved to take another city—Libnah—perhaps to set up a defensive position against a coming Egyptian force. Yet to make sure that Hezekiah doesn't try anything while he is momentarily detained, Sennacherib looks back over his shoulder and says to Hezekiah, "Don't mistake what I'm doing here. I'll be right back!" Verse 10 suggests that Sennacherib had heard about Isaiah's prophecy, and now he turns to blaspheming God. He suggests that he better knows the future and that he is more truthful than God.

Verse 11 tells us that such pride was characteristic of the Assyrian rulers. One of Sennacherib's predecessors had left this description of himself carved into the side of the old Assyrian Pass in Lebanon: "The legitimate King, King of the Universe, the King without rival, the 'great Dragon,' the only power with the four rims of the whole world who smashed all his foes like pots." I can't recall this king's name. The description sounds similar to our passage, and to the Lord's earlier reference to "the king of Assyria with all his pomp" (Isa. 8:7).

There is a lesson for us here about *pride*: beware the blinding and self-destructive effects of pride. It makes you confuse yourself with God, just as Sennacherib did.

What will happen when we confuse ourselves with God? Isaiah had answered that question earlier in his book: "The eyes of the arrogant man will be humbled and the pride of men brought low; the LORD alone will be exalted in that day" (2:11; cf 2:17; 14:12–15).

If you are not a Christian, have you ever considered how dangerous pride is? Haven't you seen how your pride hurts or even kills relationships? You would not have your job had God not given it to you. You would have not been able to do any of the good you have done were it not for God's many gifts to you of life, talent, opportunity, and time. But notice how offended you become when people don't treat you as more than you really are. Friend, humble yourself to confess your sin and repent of it, and trust in Christ.

Without him you have no hope of being born again and having a restored relationship with your Creator and Judge.

Christian, the pride left in us after conversion insults God and confuses us. It causes us to care more about what our non-Christian friends think of us than about how God will treat them in their sins. If we cared more about what God thought of our friends who don't know Christ, and cared less about what they thought about us, we would share the gospel more. If you want to grow in practicing evangelism, and for a culture of evangelism to grow up in your church, preach grace and pray for humility. It's like a spiritual superpower!

Scene #7: Hezekiah Prays to God

How would Hezekiah respond to this threat, coming now from the mighty Assyrian emperor himself?

Hezekiah received the letter from the messengers and read it. Then he went up to the temple of the LORD and spread it out before the LORD. And Hezekiah prayed to the LORD: "O LORD Almighty, God of Israel, enthroned between the cherubim, you alone are God over all the kingdoms of the earth. You have made heaven and earth. Give ear, O LORD, and hear; open your eyes, O LORD, and see; listen to all the words Sennacherib has sent to insult the living God. It is true, O LORD, that the Assyrian kings have laid waste all these people and their lands. They have thrown their gods into the fire and destroyed them, for they were not gods but only wood and stone, fashioned by human hands. Now, O LORD our God, deliver us from his hand, so that all kingdoms on earth may know that you alone, O LORD, are God." (Isa. 37:14–20)

Notice that Hezekiah begins his prayer with a wonderful and impressive statement of who God is. He next points to the fact that Sennacherib has insulted the living God. Then he draws out what was true in the words of Sennacherib. Finally he asks God for deliverance.

What does this passage have to do with evangelism? Notice in verse 20 the purpose for which Hezekiah implores God to act: "so that all kingdoms on earth may know that the LORD alone is God."

This is the point of Isaiah. More than that, this is the point of Israel's whole history. God means to make the truth about himself known. And verse 20 tells us that this remarkable story at the heart of Isaiah is all about evangelizing everyone in the world—from those on our doorstep to those at the ends of the earth.

Here's a lesson for us about *God*: Get God wrong and you will ultimately misunderstand everything else in the world. Get God right and everything else in the world will ultimately fall into the right perspective. The point of everything in life is the truth about God and his glory.

Scene #8: Isaiah Sends Hezekiah God's Word about Judah and Sennacherib

What would God do in response to Hezekiah's prayer?

Then Isaiah son of Amoz sent a message to Hezekiah: "This is what the LORD, the God of Israel, says: Because you have prayed to me concerning Sennacherib king of Assyria, this is the word the LORD has spoken against him: "The Virgin Daughter of Zion despises and mocks you. The Daughter of Jerusalem tosses her head as you flee. Who is it you have insulted and blasphemed? Against whom have you raised your voice and lifted your eyes in pride? Against the Holy One of Israel! By your

messengers you have heaped insults on the LORD. And
you have said, 'With my many chariots I have ascended
the heights of the mountains, the utmost heights of
Lebanon. I have cut down its tallest cedars, the choic-
est of its pines. I have reached its remotest heights, the
finest of its forests. I have dug wells in foreign lands and
drunk the water there. With the soles of my feet I have
dried up all the streams of Egypt.' Have you not heard?
Long ago I ordained it. In days of old I planned it; now
I have brought it to pass, that you have turned fortified
cities into piles of stone. Their people, drained of power,
are dismayed and put to shame. They are like plants in
the field, like tender green shoots, like grass sprouting on
the roof, scorched before it grows up. But I know where
you stay and when you come and go and how you rage
against me. Because you rage against me and because
your insolence has reached my ears, I will put my hook
in your nose and my bit in your mouth, and I will make
you return by the way you came. This will be the sign for
you, O Hezekiah: This year you will eat what grows by
itself, and the second year what springs from that. But
in the third year sow and reap, plant vineyards and eat
their fruit. Once more a remnant of the house of Judah
will take root below and bear fruit above. For out of
Jerusalem will come a remnant; and out of Mount Zion
a band of survivors. The zeal of the LORD Almighty will
accomplish this. Therefore this is what the LORD says
concerning the king of Assyria: He will not enter this city
or shoot an arrow here. He will not come before it with
shield or build a siege ramp against it. By the way that he
came he will return; he will not enter this city," declares

the LORD. "I will defend this city and save it, for my sake
and for the sake of David my servant!" (Isa. 37:21–35)

Sometimes Bible commentators describe chapters 36 and 37
as a hinge, or a bridge, taking us from the first half of Isaiah (with
a lot of judgment) to the second half (with a lot of hope). There is
a sense in which that's true. But even more, these chapters present us with the point of Isaiah's whole ministry. His ministry was
to prophesy and prepare and explain and instruct and utter God's
promises for even more! In that sense the rest of Isaiah—the
chapters before and after—forms a very thick frame around this
masterpiece of God's utter and complete faithfulness in a most
desperate hour. It hangs there in the hall of masterpieces of God's
love and faithfulness to his people, from Abraham to Joseph to
David and now to Hezekiah. And this hall of portraits all prepare
the way for the greatest masterpiece of all—the faithfulness of
God as seen in Jesus Christ's life, death, resurrection, and promised return for us.

Verses 22 to 29 present the LORD's answer to Sennacherib,
which he meant for Hezekiah and his people to hear and understand. He says in verse 22 that the Assyrians would flee. He asks
devastating questions in verse 23, and condemns Sennacherib for
heaping insults on him in verse 24. Then he mocks Sennacherib's
pride in verses 24 and 25.

I think the climactic verse comes in verse 26. Here God drops
the veil and offers the true interpretation of history. Sennacherib
may have boasted about all that he had done, but now God presents the bigger picture. Even a terrible event, placed in a larger
context, can look entirely different. If I told you that someone cut
my wife's neck last month, you would be horrified, at least until I
explained that it was a surgeon who was protecting her life. Satan,

of course, always wants to offer his rival interpretation of the events of our lives.

Then comes God's menacing statement in verse 28: "I know where you live, Sennacherib!" Only someone blinded by pride would not recognize the threat here. This is no local deity that Sennacherib has turned against him. In verse 29, God employs the brutal imagery of "hook in nose" that the Assyrians had used with others. Then God turns in verse 30 to giving a loving sign to Hezekiah: there will be enough food, and agriculture will soon resume.

There should be no doubt: God will completely defend Jerusalem. Why? For the sake of Hezekiah and his pious prayers? No, God will defend the city "for my sake and for the sake of David my servant" (v. 35).

Do you see the lesson here about the *sovereign God and his purposes*? The truth is that we are not that great, but God is. God alone is sovereign. God alone will fulfill his purposes.

Of course, God's people needed to know this during the Assyrian invasion, and they would need to know it when they suffered exile in Babylon, as well as when he brought them back from exile. God's people *always* need to know that God alone is sovereign and that we can trust him through the trials and tribulations that he allows in this fallen world. It was Hezekiah's faith in the sovereignty of God that led him to realize that nothing was impossible with God, that no situation was hopeless. The Lord will always be as good as his Word.

God has no peace for us to experience today apart from our faith in him, his sovereignty, and the certainty that he *will* accomplish his good purposes. Praise God for the confidence we can have in him who has not spared his own Son for us!

Scene #9: Assyrian Army Destroyed

So God promised to defeat the Assyrians and deliver his people. What happened?

> Then the angel of the LORD went out and put to death a hundred and eighty-five thousand men in the Assyrian camp. When the people got up the next morning—there were all the dead bodies! So Sennacherib king of Assyria broke camp and withdrew. He returned to Nineveh and stayed there. (Isa. 37:36–37)

The text does not say how the angel of the LORD put one hundred and eighty-five thousand Assyrian soldiers to death. But this messenger of God did it at God's command.

Of course, the Assyrian records say nothing of this. But they wouldn't, would they? Amidst all their relief sculptures, never once do they show one dead Assyrian soldier. It wouldn't fit with that almighty image they wanted to project. God had said that the Assyrians would fail, and would retreat, and so they did. God had promised earlier in the book, "I will crush the Assyrian in my land" (Isa. 14:25). And so he did.

Some wonder if God is justified in killing 185,000 people, even if they were part of a terribly brutal invading army. I have to say, from the Bible's perspective, the question is not so much why they were killed, but why we are all left alive. Our sins cry out for God's judgment. It will come unexpectedly and swiftly, Jesus taught. Therefore, Jesus said, "Be ready" (Matt. 24:24; Luke 12:40).

There is a lesson here for us on mercy: God will save and God will judge. And anything other than immediate and eternal punishment for sinners is an act of God's mercy.

Scene #10: Sennacherib's Death

The last verse of Isaiah 37 offers a postscript. It occurs fifteen to twenty years later.

> One day, while [Sennacherib] was worshiping in the temple of his god Nisroch, his sons Adrammelech and Sharezer cut him down with the sword, and they escaped to the land of Ararat. And Esarhaddon his son succeeded him as king. (v. 38)

This one who spoke like he was immortal was killed. He was killed by some of the very few humans to whom he had, in some sense, given life—his own sons. And he was killed while worshipping his god Nisroch. How sufficient, then, was the protection of this other god, particularly in contrast with Yahweh, the living God and protector of Jerusalem.

So much for human boasts!

And there is a lesson here for us about human glory: human glory is very short-lived.

I love John Wesley's reflection on human glory, penned after watching the king of England dawn his robes:

> I was in the robe-chamber, adjoining to the House of Lords, when the King put on his robes. His brow was much furrowed with age, and quite clouded with care. And is this all the world can give even to a King? All the grandeur it can afford? A blanket of ermine around his shoulders, so heavy and cumbersome he can scarce move under it! A huge heap of borrowed hair, with a few plates of gold and glittering stones upon his head! Alas, what a bauble is human greatness! And even this will not endure.[20]

Human glory is not everything it's cracked up to be. In fact, it's a cheat and a lie. Did you know that within three years of retirement, 50 percent of former NFL players are bankrupt, unemployed, and divorced? For that matter, if you ever come to visit me in Washington, DC, take notice of all the statues scattered throughout the city and see if you can identify any of them.

Still, so many people come to DC in pursuit of something that will never satisfy, and that, even if gained, can only last for such a brief time. When I came to Capitol Hill Baptist, one of our church members was one of the most powerful men in the Senate. A few years ago, when I asked the congregation, the only people who had heard of him were older members of the church. Not even the young people who worked as staffers on Capitol Hill, where this senator had been so well-known and respected, had even heard of him.

Friend, what are you spending your life on?

Conclusion

According to the Bible, we all are born "Assyrians," spiritually speaking. We all by nature oppose God. And God will judge us for it, even if our lives appear to prosper for a time in our opposition to him. The difference, of course, is that we can actually change from being Assyrians, to being adopted by God as his own special people.

Brother pastor, you need to know that God specializes in these kinds of deliverances. And to draw our eyes onto him, he will sometimes remove all the other idols that tempt us. He will turn the drawers in our lives upside down, emptying them out, so that we have nothing left to rely on but him.

And just when we think he will never do it, he delivers us! Remember that promise Jesus made: "I will build my church and the gates of Hades will not overcome it" (Matt. 16:18).

No combination of killings in Nigeria, jailings in the Middle East, and public scorn and job loss and even financial penalties in America for believing and preaching the gospel will falsify Christ's promise. None of them.

We can join Jesus in his work to build his church not only without worry that our work will be in vain, but with confidence that our evangelism will most certainly succeed in all the purposes that God intends for it.

And, brother pastors, you and I have the honor of leading Christ's church in proclaiming his glory to all people! What a privilege! What a joy!

CHAPTER 6

Inerrancy and Christ's Unbreakable Bible

Kevin DeYoung

My theme in this chapter is "Inerrancy and Christ's Unbreakable Bible." Any one of these big ideas would be big enough on its own. But I want you to see, not just how important any one of these topics is, but how important it is that they are all tied together.[21]

If we are to share the gospel with confidence and preach with authority, then we must be sure that the message we are proclaiming and the book that we are expounding are true. All true. All we have to offer the world is truth and grace. You cannot have one without the other. If you think that you can magnify grace by shrinking truth, you will find that you make people blind to both. When you teach your children about the creation of the world and Noah and the flood and Moses and the Red Sea and Jesus walking on water and Jesus casting out demons and Jesus coming back to life, when you share your faith with your skeptical neighbor, when you open the Bible to teach your hungry small group, when you stand behind the pulpit to preach the Word of God verse-by-verse, year-by-year, decade-by-decade, there is one question that towers above all others: Are you telling the truth? When you get up to preach or teach or lead your Bible study, are you telling the truth?

A Lesson in Telling (and Listening to) the Truth

Not too long ago our two oldest boys came in from the snow mired in a bit of controversy. I had barely walked into the house, just home from work, when my wife told me the tale.

"I'm so frustrated," she exclaimed. "You need to talk to the boys. Ian and Jacob were playing with their friends outside, and now Jacob is crying because the side of his face is red and icy and bruised. Ian hit him in the head with a snowball."

"Okay," I tried to say calmly, "did you talk to Ian? What did he say?"

"Well, he claims that he didn't do it. He says Jacob took a pile of snow and started rubbing it in his own face and that's how his cheek got red and icy and bruised. It's so frustrating. Why won't he just tell the truth?"

When I found Ian—our oldest child, about ten at the time—I asked him what happened. He told the same story about his eight-year-old brother rubbing snow in his own face. I said, "Really? That's hard to believe. You're telling me you didn't throw any snowballs out there?" To which Ian sheepishly replied, "I mean, I might have thrown one. But I didn't hit Jacob. Maybe my snowball bounced off a tree and landed on him."

Now I was frustrated. This was a far-fetched story. Snowballs don't normally bounce off trees. I just wanted Ian to tell me the truth. So I thought, *We are going straight to 1 John 1 for family devotions tonight*. I read the passage: "If we say we have no sin, we deceive ourselves, and the truth is not in us. If we confess our sins, he is faithful and just to forgive us our sins and to cleanse us from all unrighteousness" (vv. 8–9). We talked about sin. We talked about the deception of sin and how we lie to cover our sin. We talked about how important it is to tell the truth and confess our sins so that we can be forgiven in Christ. I had everyone go around the table and confess a sin that wanted to be forgiven. After my youngest kids took a turn, we got to my oldest son.

"Anything you want to say, Ian?" I asked.

"Um, I guess I didn't respond in a good way when Mom was upset with me because Jacob was hurt."

"Okay, that's good. Anything else you want to share?"

"No."

I sighed a little under my breath and moved on to Jacob. "Anything you want to say?" And then in an instant my eight-year-old burst into tears and blurted out, "I took the snow and rubbed it in my face!" My wife and I didn't know if we should laugh or cry. I rushed around the table and gave Jacob a big hug and told him I was proud of him for letting us know what really happened. We also told Ian we were sorry for not believing his story. Sometimes it can be hard to know what to believe. Sometimes the strangest stories are the truest. Sometimes you can't trust your own instincts. We have to listen carefully for the truth.

Because we don't have anything if we don't have the truth. This isn't about Christians claiming to have a monopoly on truth. Far from it. We want to put all the truth we have on Free Parking for anyone who wants it. We want to know the truth so we can share the truth. But how can we have the truth if we cannot trust the Scriptures? You may doubt whether you can trust a politician. You may not believe what you read on the Internet. (Good!) You may not even be sure you can trust yourself. But you can always trust the Bible. All of it. All the time, every verse, without fail, without exception, without end. Amen and Amen.

Following the Leader
(and the Book He Followed)

My aim in this chapter is simple. I want us to see what Jesus believed about the Scriptures so that we can know what we should believe about the Scriptures. We will look at four passages from the Gospels. Let's start with John 10:31–38.

> The Jews picked up stones again to stone him. Jesus answered them, "I have shown you many good works from the Father; for which of them are you going to stone me?" The Jews answered him, "It is not for a good work that we are going to stone you but for blasphemy, because you, being a man, make yourself God." Jesus answered them, "Is it not written in your Law, 'I said, you are gods'? If he called them gods to whom the word of God came—and Scripture cannot be broken—do you say of him whom the Father consecrated and sent into the world, 'You are blaspheming,' because I said, 'I am the Son of God'? If I am not doing the works of my Father, then do not believe me; but if I do them, even though you do not believe me, believe the works, that you may know and understand that the Father is in me and I am in the Father."

The Jews want to stone Jesus because, in verse 30, he has just pronounced that, "I and the Father are one." The crowds understand what some modern scholars refuse to understand. Namely, that Jesus believed himself to be divine. This makes them furious, which prompts Jesus to take them back to their own Scriptures. In particular, he quotes from Psalm 82, a little known chapter with an obscure verse about to serve an important purpose.

In order to understand what Jesus is saying, we need to understand the whole psalm.

> A Psalm of Asaph. God has taken his place in the divine
> council; in the midst of the gods he holds judgment:
> "How long will you judge unjustly and show partiality
> to the wicked? Give justice to the weak and the father-
> less; maintain the right of the afflicted and the destitute.
> Rescue the weak and the needy; deliver them from the
> hand of the wicked." They have neither knowledge nor
> understanding, they walk about in darkness; all the foun-
> dations of the earth are shaken. I said, "You are gods,
> sons of the Most High, all of you; nevertheless, like men
> you shall die, and fall like any prince." Arise, O God,
> judge the earth; for you shall inherit all the nations!

This is a strange psalm and Jesus pulls from it a strange verse. He quotes the line "I said you are gods." The Hebrew word there is *elohim*, which usually means God, but can mean gods. Here the psalmist is not thinking of divine beings per se. He uses the word in reference to kings or judges or magistrates. Jesus is not trying to prove his divinity from this one psalm, rather he is trying to puncture their pretentions. He says in effect, "Look, you're hung up on the word 'God,' that I say I'm the Son of God. But don't you remember in your own Law how these princes and these wicked rulers were called 'gods.'" Jesus doesn't think these rulers were divine beings, but they were in their positions by divine appointment and wielded divinely given authority. And if they can be called "gods" (in some sense of the word), why not the Christ?

The reason to spend time in Psalm 82 and take the effort to understand Jesus' argument is so we can get to the comment he makes in John 10:35: "Scripture cannot be broken." Jesus can make this remark almost as an aside because he knew it was uncontroversial. This was the common ground he shared with opponents. They may have debated the deity of Christ, but no Jew would have denied the utter trustworthiness of Scripture. It's really remarkable what Jesus is doing. The divine Son of God has no hesitancy in arguing a point based on one word from a confusing verse in an out of the way psalm. Jesus is not quoting from one of the great passages in Exodus or one of the great servant songs in Isaiah. Jesus does not even bother to prove that this psalm or this verse or this word is authoritative. Its authority was unquestioned because it was a part of their Bible. As one commentator put it, "It was sufficient proof of the infallibility of any sentence or phrase or clause to show that it constituted a portion of what the Jews called the Scripture."[22]

And Jesus said the Scripture cannot be broken. The Greek word is *luo*. It's the same word we'll see in a moment in Matthew 5:18–19 where Jesus warns against relaxing (*luo*) or annulling or breaking or loosing or nullifying or setting aside any little jot or tittle of Scripture. For Jesus, no word in his Bible could be falsified. No promise or threat could fall short of fulfillment. No statement could be found guilty of error.

The Scriptures could not be broken because they were the very words of God. And who would dare suggest that a word committed to writing by Almighty God could be an errant word, a wrong word, or a broken word? Such a thing would not have been a sign of enlightenment to Jesus, but a sign of blasphemy. There was no debate in Jesus' day about the authority of Scripture. How could Scripture be broken if Scripture was God himself speaking?

It's also worth noting that Jesus believed this unbreakable word was an understandable word. We all know this intuitively but we don't often think of the implications. Dozens of times Jesus appeals to a text from the Old Testament thinking that such an appeal constitutes a strong argument on his side. He assumed that the Old Testament was not only authoritative, but that it possessed a shared, discernible meaning. Jesus often cites the Scriptures as evidence for his teaching. Other times he chides the Jews for not conforming to the Word of God. Six times Jesus says, "Have you not read?" suggesting that if they knew the Scriptures they would not be making the mistakes they were making. The apostles did the same thing—quoting from the Scriptures, reasoning from the Scriptures, alluding to the Scriptures—all with the assumption that these texts said what was true and the truth that they communicated could be understood. Reader response theory would have been very strange to Jesus. He believed that the Word of God—though it would take the illuminating work of the Spirit to really appropriate what it says—could be understood even by his opponents.

Are you familiar with the fable about the six blind men and the elephant? In this little doggerel you have six blind men groping around in the darkness trying to figure out what they are feeling. One of them touches the elephant's side and says it's a wall. One of them pulls on his tail and says it's a rope. One of them pulls on his ear and says it's a fan. And on and on. The point of the fable is that this is what we are all like in religion. We think we know God but we are just feeling our way in the darkness, all thinking that the part of the truth we've encountered gives the ability to pontificate about the whole thing. We all have our theories. We all have our interpretations. We all have our ideas. But in the end we are just blind men who can't see the elephant.

It's a nice analogy, but I hope you can see two colossal problems with the fable. One, the analogy is told from the position of omniscience. There is someone who knows the complete truth of the situation, enough to know that the elephant is really an elephant and the men are really blind. The story doesn't work except in the context of absolute truth. The other problem is that the whole analogy breaks down if the elephant speaks. The elephant in the story doesn't say anything. He just stands there silently as blind men try to figure out what they are feeling. But what if the elephant says, "Hello, I'm not a fan. I'm not a wall. I'm not a rope. I'm an elephant." Then what? Should we call it a paradox? Or a cloud of unknowing? Or have a conference about what to make of these new sounds? If the elephant speaks, all our talk of chastened epistemology is less a sign of humility than a sign that we are hard of hearing. The Jesus we meet in John 10 is a Jesus utterly confident in the Scripture and utterly confident that the Scriptures communicate truth that humans can understand and should accept.

Pharisaic Legalism or Christlike Loyalty?

For our second text let's look at Matthew 5:17–19. Jesus says Scripture cannot be broken in John 10, and he says much the same thing in this famed passage from the Sermon on the Mount.

> "Do not think that I have come to abolish the Law or the
> Prophets; I have not come to abolish them but to fulfill
> them. For truly, I say to you, until heaven and earth pass
> away, not an iota, not a dot, will pass from the Law until
> all is accomplished. Therefore whoever relaxes one of the
> least of these commandments and teaches others to do
> the same will be called least in the kingdom of heaven,

but whoever does them and teaches them will be called great in the kingdom of heaven."

It's important to note from the beginning that Jesus is talking about more than the kerygmatic event. In neo-orthodoxy the authority was in the Word of God, but it was the Word of God as it comes to us by the Spirit in preaching or through the proclamation of the gospel. Neo-orthodoxy tries to distance the locus of authority from the written text. But here Jesus clearly has in mind written Scripture. We know this is the case because he references an iota, the smallest letter in the alphabet, and a dot, the tiniest stroke of the pen. Jesus did not come to abolish or relax the smallest speck of Scripture, not the most miniscule marking.

Throughout the Sermon on the Mount, especially in chapter 5, Jesus presses home the truest and fullest meaning of Scripture. To be sure, he will gladly undermine the false traditions of the scribes and Pharisees. He will even correct their false *interpretations* of Scripture. But he will never allow the Word of God to be circumvented by tradition or self-justifying circumlocutions. Every speck is true, unbreakable, and must be applied to our lives. As Donald Macleod puts it, "For Jesus, jot-and-tittle loyalty to Scripture is neither legalistic nor evasive. . . . Jot-and-tittle fulfillment of the law means avoiding anger as well as homicide; lust as well as fornication; swearing as well as perjury. It means turning the other cheek, going the extra mile, blowing no trumpets when we make donations for charity."[23]

Do you remember what Jesus says in Matthew 23:23? He's denouncing the scribes and Pharisees for their hypocrisy; and in the midst of all these woes, Jesus criticizes the religious leaders for tithing their little spices but neglecting the weightier matters of the law like justice, mercy, and faithfulness. Sounds like something Jesus would say, except don't miss *exactly* what Jesus communicates. He says, "These you ought to have done, without neglecting the others." Jesus didn't think that it was legalistic to obey the little details in the law. He wasn't just interested in the big picture or the biggest commandments. He expected obedience to the spirit and to the letter of the law. Of course, there are redemptive historical things going on where elements of the Mosaic dispensation will find their fullest expression in Christ. Obedience to the law is transformed by the coming of Christ. But his coming never meant a "whatever" attitude toward the Scriptures. Jesus shows familiarity with every kind of Scripture and references it all as equally true, authoritative, and never to be ignored.

The Facts of History

Turn over a few more chapters to Matthew 12:38–42. This is our third of four passages I want us to look at.

> Then some of the scribes and Pharisees answered him, saying, "Teacher, we wish to see a sign from you." But he answered them, "An evil and adulterous generation seeks for a sign, but no sign will be given to it except the sign of the prophet Jonah. For just as Jonah was three days and three nights in the belly of the great fish, so will the Son of Man be three days and three nights in the heart of the earth. The men of Nineveh will rise up at the judgment with this generation and condemn it, for they repented at the preaching of Jonah, and behold, something greater than Jonah is here. The queen of the South will rise up at the judgment with this generation and condemn it, for she came from the ends of the earth to hear the wisdom of Solomon, and behold, something greater than Solomon is here."

Jesus consistently treats biblical history as a narrative of facts. He makes references to Abel, Noah, Abraham, Sodom and Gomorrah, Isaac and Jacob, manna in the wilderness, the serpent in the wilderness, Moses, David, Solomon, the Queen of Sheba, Elijah, Elisha, the widow of Zarephath, Naaman, Jonah, and Zechariah, without ever questioning a single story, a single miracle, or a single historical claim. This story about Jonah is the one that is hardest for some people to swallow (pun intended). People will say, "Look, this is clearly just an allusion to a bit of Israel folklore. Jesus doesn't think that an actual prophet lived in the belly of an actual fish. He's simply referencing the story much like we might make a passing reference to Aslan breaking the Stone Table or to the orcs of Mordor. Jesus accepted the stories of the Old Testament, but that doesn't mean he thought the stories were meant to be taken as literal history."

This interpretation sounds plausible until you look more closely at the details. Jesus also mentions in this paragraph the Queen of Sheba, demonstrable a historical person. He then says that the men of Nineveh will rise up in judgment against Capernaum on the last day. How does this work if the story of Jonah is as historically accurate as Paul Bunyan and Babe the Blue Ox? Jesus must be talking about the real people of Nineveh. If I were to say to you, with a sense of dire warning, that you must repent lest the men of Gondor rise up against you, that might be a cool, nerdy thing to say, but it wouldn't be taken seriously as a threat of judgment because the men of Gondor don't really exist (sorry to break it to you). T. T. Perowne asks a good question about Jesus' use of the Jonah story: "Are we to suppose him to say that imaginary persons who at the preaching of an imaginary prophet repented in imagination, shall rise up in that day and condemn the actual impenitence of those his actual hearers?"[24] Isn't it better to conclude that Jesus believed the story of Jonah actually happened in all its wonderful, miraculous detail?

If Jesus is right in his straightforward acceptance of Old Testament history, then boatloads—Titanic loads in fact—of modern biblical criticism must be wrong. For the past 150 to 200 years many modern scholars have argued that the Old Testament is far different than what it seems. The first five books were not written by Moses, but were the product of an elaborate combination of different sources, some of which are a thousand years later than Moses. Isaiah was not written by Isaiah but by two Isaiahs, or maybe three Isaiahs, whose stunning predictions were not actually predictions but after-the-fact pronouncements. If liberal scholars are right, the church misread Israel's history for almost two millennia. Israel's story was not about centuries of struggle to be faithful to the One True God and obey his law. What took place instead, they say, was a kind of evolutionary development. Israel moved from animism to polytheism to henotheism (worshiping one god among many existing gods) to monotheism, and finally to the triumph of priestly legalism. Books that claim to be from the Exodus are later than Ezekiel. First Samuel, which was thought to be written after the giving of the law, actually describes Israel before the law. The Pentateuch, instead of being the foundation for Israel's life, actually came after the glory days were far behind her. This is part and parcel of what seems plain to so much modern scholarship and is not remotely connected to anything we see from Jesus in how he handled the Hebrew Scriptures.

Jesus believed Israel was, during its long history, under the tutelage of Yahweh. He believed that Moses gave a national covenant to live by, that the Pentateuch came at the beginning of their history, that the prophets rebuked and refined Israel for their failures. If the revisionist history is correct, Jesus was monumentally wrong in believing all this. This is not about carrying water for some newfangled doctrine of inerrancy invented by Old Princeton. If all of the liberal theories are right, we don't just lose Hodge or Warfield, we're going to lose Jesus. For Jesus did not realize that Leviticus was a betrayal of ethical monotheism. He was unaware of the composite authorship of the Pentateuch. He completely misread Israel's history. The Son of God was taken in by a national myth no more plausible than that of Romulus and Remus.[25]

Is it not plausible to think—dare we say quite likely— that Jesus knew Jewish history better than nineteenth-century Germans? Isn't it safer to side with Jesus and his supremely high view of inspiration and his straightforward understanding of history and chronology? Jesus not only believed the Scriptures could not be broken and that every jot and tittle were from God himself, but he approached the Scriptures believing the chronology was chronological, the history was historical, and the authors of the biblical books were who the Jews thought them to be.

The Greeks and Romans had lots of myths, and they didn't particularly care whether Hercules was really the illegitimate son of Zeus. It was a fable, a tall tale. It was meant to explain the world. This is entirely different from Christianity and Judaism. In the Judeo-Christian worldview, history matters. Several years ago around Christmastime I wrote a blog about the importance of the virgin birth. Another minister, one who was a part of my denomination at the time, took issue with some of my points. He thought that we didn't have to believe in the virgin birth. He believed Matthew and Isaiah may have been talking about a young woman, not a literal virgin. Finally, after going back and forth a bit, he landed his final blow:

> Do I think the virgin birth is essential to our creed as
> Christians? That's not really mine to say, is it? As you say,
> it has been confessed for centuries and thus, I need to

take it seriously and to wrestle with how I understand it. For my part, I take the statement to Mary "all things are possible with God" as more valuable to my faith than the statement "how can this be since I am still a virgin?" I don't claim that you need to accept my understanding nor would I imagine that you would claim that I must necessarily accept your understanding.

To which I replied, as graciously as I could, "I do, in fact, think you need to accept my understanding of the virgin birth, not because it is my understanding but it is the record of the holy Gospel writers inspired by the Holy Spirit, and it has been the record of the church universal throughout the centuries." The man's words sounded humble, but they have no place among those who have been called to teach God's Word. If you are a fifteen-year-old or a first-year seminary student and you are wrestling with the virgin birth, then by all means let us have remarkable patience. But James 3:1 says not many of you should be teachers for you will be judged more strictly. God doesn't expect us simply to wrestle with what he says in the Bible or to take the truths of Scripture seriously. He expects us to believe them, and he expects ministers to preach them. If it's so important to us that "all things are possible with God" (Mark 10:27) why would we doubt that he can do seemingly impossible things like causing a virgin to conceive and give birth to our Messiah?

This cannot be stated too strongly: Christianity, from the very beginning, tied itself to history. The most important claims of Christianity are historical claims. And on this history, Christianity must rise or fall. If Jesus has not risen from the dead, Christianity is a great hoax and you are of all people most to be pitied. Pack it in. Sleep in. Enjoy football. Do something else on Sunday morning if the Gospels aren't history. Because the New Testament tells us there was a man who began his life as a baby born of a woman in Bethlehem. Thousands of people saw him and knew him. He did miracles witnessed by multitudes. He died and rose again and appeared to more than five hundred witnesses at one time. Everyone knew the location of his tomb and could see for themselves that it was empty. Three disciples were eye-witnesses of his majesty on the mountain. They saw redemptive history unfold before their eyes and the Spirit inspired them to record it. We do not follow myths. We are not interested in stories with a nice moral to them. We are not helped by hoping in spiritual possibilities. These things in the Gospels happened. God predicted them. He fulfilled them. He inspired the written record of them. To discount history is to live in a different world than the ones that the biblical authors inhabited.

Scripture Says What God Says

Let's look at one final passage, Matthew 19:3–6.

And Pharisees came up to him [that is, to Jesus] and tested him by asking, "Is it lawful to divorce one's wife for any cause?" He answered, "Have you not read that he who created them from the beginning made them male and female, and said, 'Therefore a man shall leave his father and his mother and hold fast to his wife, and the two shall become one flesh'? So they are no longer two but one flesh. What therefore God has joined together, let not man separate."

In order to understand the monumental significance of Jesus' assumption here, we need see what Genesis does and does not say. Jesus is quoting in verse 5 from Genesis 2:24. And who exactly is he quoting? Well, no one in particular. There is no specific author assigned to Genesis 2:24; it's simply part of the narration. But notice what Jesus says in Matthew 19:4. The one who created the man and the woman is the one who uttered the statement about the two becoming one flesh. In other words, according to Christ, Genesis 2:24 was spoken by the Creator. Jesus understood, as any Jew would have, that to quote from a verse in Scripture was to quote from God himself.

Jesus has no problem referencing human authors like Moses, Isaiah, David, and Daniel. But they stand in the background. They are the sub-authors doing the work of the Divine Author who inspired their words. This is why Mark 12:36 refers to David speaking in the Holy Spirit; and Hebrews quotes from Scripture saying "the Holy Spirit says"; and Romans 9:17 quotes from God saying "the Scripture says to Pharaoh"; and Galatians 3:8 can say "the Scripture . . . preached the gospel beforehand to Abraham." Jesus and the apostles do not hesitate to use "God" and "Scripture" interchangeably. Their authority is the same because God is the Author of Scripture and Scripture is the Word of God. Before we think it a mark of our sophistication to minimize or somehow weaken the authority of Scripture, we should remember that our Lord Jesus Christ, the perfect son of man and Son of God, when he was tempted by the devil, did not draw down on superpowers or shoot lightning bolts from his eyes. When confronted by temptation in the wilderness, three times he quoted Deuteronomy to the devil. "It is written" was sufficient for Jesus, and it should be enough for us.

For Jesus, Scripture is powerful, decisive, and authoritative because it is the voice of God. It is as true as God is true. I have little patience for those who want to pit the Word (Christ) against the Word (the Bible). God's gracious self-disclosure comes to us through the Word made flesh and by the inscripturated Word of God. These two modes of revelation reveal to us one God, one truth, one way, and one coherent set of promises, threats, and commands. Of course, we do not identify the actual artifacts of ink and paper and binding as somehow being divine. But we must not seek to know the Word who is divine apart from the divine words of the Bible, and we ought not read the words of the Bible without an eye to the Word incarnate. When it comes to seeing God and his truth in Christ and in Holy Scripture, one is not more reliable, more trustworthy, or more relevant than the other. Scripture, because it is the breathed-out Word of God, possesses the same authority as the God-man Jesus Christ. Submission to the Scriptures is submission to God. Rebellion against the Scriptures is rebellion against God. The Bible can no more fail, falter, or err than God himself can fail, falter, or err. Scripture must be inerrant because Scripture is the Word of God and God is inerrant.

Inerrancy means the Word of God always stands over us and we never stand over the Word of God. When we reject inerrancy we put ourselves in judgment over God's Word. We claim the right to determine which parts of God's revelation can be trusted and which cannot. When we deny the complete trustworthiness of the Scriptures—in its genuine claims with regard to history, its teachings on the material world, its miracles, in the tiniest jots and tittles of all that it affirms—then we are forced to accept one of two conclusions. Either the Scripture is not all from God, or God is not always dependable. To make either statement is to affirm what is sub-Christian. These conclusions do not express a proper submission to the Father, do not work for our joy in Christ, and do not bring honor to the Spirit, who carried along the men to speak the prophetic word and author God's holy book.

Finding a halfway house where some things in the Bible are true and other things (as we have judged them) are not is an impossibility. This kind of compromised Christianity, besides flying in the face of the Bible's own self-understanding, does not satisfy the soul or present to the lost the sort of God they need to meet. How are we to believe in a God who can do the unimaginable and forgive our trespasses, conquer our sins, and give us hope in a dark world if we cannot believe that this God created the world out of nothing, gave the virgin a child, and raised his Son on the third day? "One cannot doubt the Bible," J. I. Packer warns, "without far-reaching loss, both of fullness of truth and of fullness of life. If therefore we have at heart spiritual renewal for society, for churches and for our own lives, we shall make much of the entire trustworthiness—that is, the inerrancy—of Holy Scripture as the inspired and liberating Word of God."[26]

We are sometimes told that the final authority for us as Christians should be Christ and not the Scriptures. It is suggested that Christ would have us accept only the portions of Scripture that comport with his life and teaching, that certain aspects of biblical history, chronology, and cosmology need not bother us because Christ would not have us be bothered by them. The idea put forward by many liberal Christians and not a few self-proclaimed evangelicals is that if we are to worship Christ and not the Scriptures, we must let Christ stand apart from Scripture and above it. "But who is this Christ, the Judge of Scripture?" Packer asks. "Not the Christ of the New Testament and of history. That Christ does not judge Scripture; He obeys it and fulfills it. By word and deed He endorses the authority of the whole of it."[27]

Those with a high view of Scripture may be charged with idolatry for so deeply reverencing the Word of God. But the accusation is laid at the wrong feet. Packer observes,

> A Christ who permits His followers to set Him up as
> the Judge of Scripture, one by whom its authority must
> be confirmed before it becomes binding and by whose

adverse sentence it is in places annulled, is a Christ of human imagination, made in the theologian's own image, One whose attitude to Scripture is the opposite of that of the Christ of history. If the construction of such a Christ is not a breach of the second commandment, it is hard to see what is.[28]

Jesus may have seen himself as the focal point of Scripture, but never as a judge of it. The only Jesus who stands above Scripture is the Jesus of our own invention.

Rubber, Say Hello to the Road

Here's where things get most practical for those of us in full-time ministry. As you stand behind the pulpit to preach—verse by verse, year after year, decade after decade—what will your people sense is the final word? You or the Bible? Their experience or the Bible? Peer review journals or the Bible? Their sense of God's own inner workings and their soul or the Bible? Biology or the Bible? Cultural acceptance or the Bible? What will you and your people trust completely and unreservedly? As the issue of sexuality continues to rage on in our culture, I've said to my people from time to time something like this: "You need to resolve in your own mind and heart right now, on this morning, in the relative safety of this place, surrounded by people you know and love, worshipping God together—you need to decide now whether you will stand on this Word or some other word. And you need to decide it now. Will you trust this Word? Do you believe this Word? Is this book true though every man call it a liar (or worse)?" In the pulpit and in the pew, we must not waver in our confidence in the trustworthiness of Scripture.

Is everything in the Bible, taken in context and interpreted correctly, all true? If not, then you will need to correct, qualify, and come to the task of teaching and evangelism somewhat cowardly. But if it is all true, you can come with confidence. You can have boldness, which is not a personality type, or arrogance, or bravado. To be bold is to be clear in the face of fear. It is to say with confidence what people may not want to hear because you know that God has already said it.

Do you remember what happens at the end of the Sermon on the Mount? The crowds marveled at Jesus' teaching. And why? Because he was so clever? Because he was really, really hilarious? Because he had multiple degrees? Because he had a large following? They marveled because Jesus, unlike the scribes and the Pharisees, spoke as one who had authority.

I own all seven volumes of Hughes Old's magisterial series on *The Reading and Preaching of the Scriptures in the Worship of the Christian Church.*[29] At more than four thousand pages I haven't read everything in every volume, but what I've read has been consistently edifying and fascinating. For the most part, Old finds something to like in most preachers. (It would be hard to write four thousand words if you disliked most of what you were reading and hearing.) But he does not like everything in the history of Christian preaching. On a sermon from Harry Emerson Fosdick, the liberal's liberal, Old writes, "One can well imagine that his congregation was completely satisfied that their preacher had made the doctrine of the divinity of Christ personally relevant. Others, however, might wonder if the God who is totally other had in fact been totally ignored."[30] About Norman Vincent Peale, the popular preacher of positive thinking, Old says, "The embarrassing thing about his ministry is that he won such an enormous following preaching from the pulpit of such a historic church."[31] And later (and worse): "We know that Peale never made any attempt to expound a text of Scripture in his sermons."[32]

Old is not a cheerleader for any and every kind of preaching. In general, he is most enthusiastic about expositional, evangelical preaching. Which is why his comments on John MacArthur are so curious and so illuminating at the same time. Old notices time and again how MacArthur never "has the least shadow of doubt but that these miracles took place exactly as they are recorded." He comments, perceptively, that MacArthur has no interest in defending the accuracy of the Bible. "He simply assumes it is all quite reliable. This basic assumption that the text of Scripture is reliable is part of the foundation of his effectiveness as an interpreter."[33]

One gets the impression that while listening to MacArthur's sermons, Old is forced to wrestle with his own view of Scripture and the supernatural:

> The place where I have always had the greatest trouble is the whole matter of exorcism. I really do not believe in Satan, demonic spirits, and demon possession. Maybe I ought to, but I don't. I am willing to agree that I may have been too strongly influenced by the intellectual world in which I was brought up to fully grasp the full teaching of Scripture, but that is the way it is. What is more than clear to me after listening to these sermons is that those who can take the text the way it is seem to make a lot more sense of it than those who are always trying to second-guess it. Surely one of the greatest strengths of MacArthur's preaching ministry is his complete confidence in the text.[34]

I was surprised and saddened by this paragraph, but I suppose Old is at least being honest. It's safe to say MacArthur isn't the ultimate example of preaching for Old, and yet he is mesmerized by his simple allegiance to the text and the sense of divine authority that comes as a result. When he comes to summarize

MacArthur's preaching, it's as if he can only find one thing he likes about it.

> Why do so many people listen to MacArthur, this prod-
> uct of all the wrong schools? How can he pack out a
> church on Sunday morning in an age in which church
> attendance has seriously lagged? Here is a preacher who
> has nothing in the way of a winning personality, good
> looks, or charm. Here is a preacher who offers us noth-
> ing in the way of sophisticated homiletical packaging. No
> one would suggest that he is a master of the art of ora-
> tory. What he seems to have is a witness to true author-
> ity. He recognizes in Scripture the Word of God, and
> when he preaches, it is Scripture that one hears. It is not
> that the words of John MacArthur are so interesting as it
> is that the Word of God is of surpassing interest. That is
> why one listens.[35]

And all the plain-looking, personally dull, oratorically defi-cient stick-to-the-Bible-and-nothing-but-the-Bible preachers said, "Amen." Pastors, do you believe that the Word of God is sufficient to do the work of God? Do you really believe that? If you don't, you will have gimmicks and gadgets and you will try to be clever and find tricks. Do you really know that you have nothing in your arsenal except for the Word of God and prayer? And if you know how to grow your church apart from the Word of God and prayer, then don't bother growing it because it may not be a church you are growing. We have no gimmicks, no gadgets, no clever tricks. Nothing on our side except the Word of God and prayer. And it is more than enough.

Say It Like You Mean It, and Believe It Like Jesus

The world dislikes so much of what you have to say. It positively hates that you would be so sure about saying it. You can say almost anything you want, if it doesn't seem like you mean it. You can say the hardest things, if everyone can tell you are hardly sure about anything you are saying. The challenge of evangelism and the challenge of preaching in our day are twofold: whether we dare to say what God's Word says, and whether we dare to say this truth as if God himself has said it. The work of evangelism is grounded in the doctrine of inerrancy, which is rooted in Christ's own commitment to the Scriptures.

Jesus held Scripture in the highest esteem. He knew his Bible intimately and loved it deeply. He often spoke with the language of Scripture. He easily alluded to Scripture. And in his moments of greatest trial and weakness—like being tempted by the devil or being crucified on a cross—he quoted Scripture. His mission was to fulfill Scripture. His teaching always upheld Scripture. He never disrespected, never disregarded, never disagreed with a single text of Scripture. He affirmed every bit of law, prophecy, narrative, and poetry. He never, for a moment, accepted the legitimacy of anyone, anywhere violating, ignoring, refining, or rejecting Scripture. He would not have re-tweeted them. He would have not have applauded them for being authentic, nor published their books, nor invited them to speak in an effort to further the conversation.

Jesus believed in the inspiration of Scripture, all of it. He accepted the chronology, the miracles, the authorial ascriptions. He believed in keeping the spirit of the law without ever minimizing the letter of the law. He affirmed the human authorship of Scripture while at the same time bearing witness to the divine authorship of Scripture. He treated the Bible as a necessary word, a sufficient word, a clear word, and the final word. It was never acceptable, in the mind of our Savior, to contradict Scripture or stand above Scripture.

He believed the Bible was all true, all edifying, all important, and all about him. He believed absolutely that the Bible was from God and absolutely free from error. What Scripture says, God says, and what God said has been recorded infallibly in Scripture.

Well, are we then just guilty of bibliolatry? Nonsense. It is impossible to revere the Scriptures more deeply or affirm them more completely than Jesus did. Jesus submitted his will to the Scriptures. He committed his brain to studying the Scriptures. He humbled his heart to obey the Scriptures. The Lord Jesus Christ, God's Son, our Savior believed the Bible was the Word of God down to the sentences, to the phrases, to the words, to the smallest letter, to the tiniest speck. And that nothing in all those specks and in all those books, in all of his holy Bible, could ever be broken.

Thus he spoke, and so should we. With truth, with grace, with joy, and with utter confidence and unashamed hope.

CHAPTER 7

Jesus Makes the Unclean Clean
(Numbers 5:1–4)

J. Ligon Duncan

✝ Numbers. The book with the worst title in the English Bible. "In the wilderness," the book's Hebrew title, would be an improvement. Steven Spielberg could do something with that, but "Numbers" only the math majors could love. Furthermore, Numbers doesn't usually rank highly on our lists of favorite Bible books. John. Romans. The Psalms. Even Genesis. But few would even put Numbers in their top ten.

Thirty-six chapters; 1,288 verses; lots of laws; lots of sand; lots of desert; lots of grumbling; lots of wandering—it doesn't sound very hopeful, does it? But do not underestimate this book. It is the Word of God, and "All Scripture is breathed out by God and profitable for teaching" (2 Tim. 3:16). I want you to see how important, practical, applicable, and profitable the book of Numbers is. I want to preach to you the gospel by Numbers.

The Challenges of Numbers

Before we begin, I want to highlight a number of things about the book of Numbers that modern readers find challenging. I'll mention three: history, bad behavior, and obscure laws.

First of all, it's a book of history, and some folk's eyes glaze over when they hear the word "history." Contemporary Americans have often failed to see the value of history. Our patron saint, Henry Ford, once said, "History is bunk." Similarly, this is why one British scholar wryly opined, "War is God's way of teaching Americans history and geography." Now, I love history. I'm from Mississippi, a state where a man once said, "The past isn't dead, it isn't even past." But even if you don't love history, you've never read history like Moses can tell it. And, after all, this is the story of your people. If you are a believer, this is *your* story. This is your family history.

Second, Numbers can be a depressing book because it records the story of God's people behaving badly. In this way, they were like us, and even though we'd rather not read about ourselves behaving badly nor think about our sin, it's important that we do. It's important that we think about it, that we deal with it, and that we repent of it. And this book helps us do that. This is one of the applications of Numbers that the New Testament explicitly makes to Christians.

Third, this book is filled with strange and bizarre laws and rituals that may seem impenetrable, irrelevant, and unconnected to the more exciting history of God's people in their wilderness wanderings. But Moses is a great storyteller, and the laws, procedures, and rituals he records are actually connected with a divine logic to the story he tells. They explain to us things we need to know about God, about ourselves, and about our Savior.

The New Testament Teaches that Christians Are to Be Instructed by Numbers

If you're wondering whether this book is worth the effort, I want to remind you that the apostle Paul explicitly tells us in 1 Corinthians 10:1–13 that the wilderness events in Exodus and Numbers happened and were written down for us. Numbers is a Christian book. Even its ceremonial laws—laws that are no longer binding on believers (Mark 7:19; Acts 15:5–10; Heb. 9:8–14; 10:1–10)—are filled with lessons for Christians. This book is meant to teach Christians about the Christian life. And I didn't make that up. Paul said it:

> For I do not want you to be unaware, brothers, that our fathers were all under the cloud, and all passed through the sea, and all were baptized into Moses in the cloud and in the sea, and all ate the same spiritual food, and all drank the same spiritual drink. For they drank from the spiritual Rock that followed them, and the Rock was Christ. Nevertheless, with most of them God was not pleased, for they were overthrown in the wilderness.
>
> *Now these things took place as examples for us,* that we might not desire evil as they did. Do not be idolaters as some of them were; as it is written, "The people sat down to eat and drink and rose up to play." We must not indulge in sexual immorality as some of them did, and twenty-three thousand fell in a single day. We must not put Christ to the test, as some of them did and were destroyed by serpents, nor grumble, as some of them did and were destroyed by the Destroyer. Now these things

happened to them as an example, but they were written down for our instruction, on whom the end of the
ages has come. Therefore let anyone who thinks that he
stands take heed lest he fall. No temptation has over-
taken you that is not common to man. God is faithful,
and he will not let you be tempted beyond your ability,
but with the temptation he will also provide the way of
escape, that you may be able to endure it. (1 Cor. 10:1–
13, emphasis added)

Don't miss what Paul says in verse 6: the events recorded in
Exodus and Numbers took place as *examples* for us. What happened to and with our Hebrew forebearers was, by God's design
and providence, meant to be an example to us as Christians more
than three thousand years later. And then in verse 11 Paul says
they happened as an example and were *written down* for us. Paul
says the very reason that God had Moses write this history was for
us! So, these things, this story, these laws are meant to instruct us.
We should pay close attention to them.

Now I want to direct your attention to a seemingly obscure and
initially baffling example of the laws recorded by Moses. Consider
Numbers 5:1–4:

Then the LORD spoke to Moses, saying, "Command the
sons of Israel that they send away from the camp every
leper and everyone having a discharge and everyone who
is unclean because of a dead person. You shall send away
both male and female; you shall send them outside the
camp so that they will not defile their camp where I
dwell in their midst."

And the sons of Israel did so and sent them outside
the camp; just as the Lord had spoken to Moses, thus
the sons of Israel did. (NASB)

It seems hard, doesn't it? You are a faithful Israelite. You love God. You are grateful that he has redeemed you out of the land of Egypt, out of the house of bondage. You are traveling with his people in the wilderness on the way to the Promised Land. You believe Moses' word. You worship the living God. You have turned your back on idolatry, but you have become defiled through no fault of your own. You're a man or a woman and you have a discharge—and so you are expelled from the camp of God.

Or, you've contracted leprosy. The first five books of the Bible cover skin diseases all the way up to and including the dreaded Hansen's disease with the term "leprosy." Some of them are permanent, some of them are temporary, and if you've contracted that skin disease it's not your fault. But you are excluded from the camp.

Or, as we will see in Leviticus 15:1–13, you've come into contact with someone with a skin disease or a discharge and so you're excluded from the camp. Or, what's worse, someone you love has died and you've come into contact with the dead body of your loved one and so you're expelled from the camp. That seems hard. It seems like God's not very loving, caring, or kind. What is going on in these laws? Why would God command this? What is he teaching us?

Well, notice three things. These laws have a practical function, a theological function, and a Christological function. That is, they have a practical purpose: God is actually caring for his people lovingly by giving these seemingly hard commands. They have a theological purpose: they teach us something important about God. And, most importantly of all, these laws point us to Jesus.

The Practical Purpose of the Laws in Numbers

These laws have a practical purpose. Far from being cruel, unreasonable, and uncaring, these laws actually show God's attentive, wise, and pastoral care for his people. How so, you ask? Well, hundreds of thousands of people are in the desert with minimal medical resources, and certainly nothing like our modern antibiotics, which are themselves an expression of the kindness of God's common grace to us all. In their context, in their situation and circumstances, contact with a dreaded skin disease, some kinds of bodily discharges, or a dead body could have spread an epidemic that could have killed tens of thousands of people. The only way to deal with that was by quarantine. As hard as that may seem, God in his kindness is taking care of hundreds of thousands of people by providing them these stipulations. He's caring for both the sick and those who come into direct contact with them by demanding the removal of the sick from the proximity of those who are well. God always has his purposes. They may seem hard, but they are good, right, and wise—and, ultimately, when we see the big picture, they are kind.

But, as Calvin observes, God was not simply acting as a physician here, he had something more important to teach us in these laws.

The Theological Purpose of
the Laws in Numbers

These laws were given for a theological reason. They were actually given to teach the people of Israel about who God is and what he is like. They draw attention to an important attribute of God, one of the great blessings he has granted to his people, and one of his great activities as God. In short, they were designed to teach the children of Israel that God is holy, that God is present, and that God has spoken.

God Is Holy—"that they may not defile their camp, in . . . which I dwell" (5:3)

The defilement laws of Numbers and Leviticus speak of a God who is undefiled and who does not dwell with those who are defiled. He is holy. The fundamental meaning of that word is that he is separate from that which is defiled.

We see that language even here in Numbers 5:1–4. Why are they to be sent away? Verse 3, "so that they may not defile the camp in . . . which I dwell." God is without defilement. God dwells in the camp. Those who are defiled must go outside the camp.

Understand that in the Law of Moses there are many ways that the doctrine of sin is taught. Sin, in the Torah, the instruction from God through Moses, is transgression, breaking the law of God. In the language of the *Westminster Shorter Catechism*, which is simply echoing and elaborating on 1 John 3:4, "sin is any want of conformity unto, or transgression of, the law of God." That is, you can transgress God's law in two ways. You can not do what he tells you to do, or you can do what he tells you not to do. Either way, you are transgressing the law, and sin is explained repeatedly as transgression in the books of Moses (e.g., Gen. 50:17; Exod. 23:21; 34:7; Num. 14:18).

Sin is also explained as defilement. It defiles you. It brings about in you that which God did not intend when he created human beings. And the ultimate expression and consequence of that defilement is death. Adam and Eve thought they would get equality with God and life by transgressing his law. Instead, they got defilement and death. Over and over in Numbers and Leviticus, in particular, sin is pictured for us as defilement, and in these laws of exclusion we get a graphic picture of what defilement does to our communion with a holy God. Just as Adam and Eve, after their sin, were excluded from the garden and the company of the holy God, so those who are ritually defiled in Israel are excluded from the camp where the holy and undefiled God is. Adam and Eve's sin in the garden was, at least in part, idolatry—they worshiped their own wills rather than obeying God and they wanted to be equal with him—and throughout the Old Testament idolatry is said to entail defilement (e.g., Isa. 30:22; Jer. 7:30; 32:34).

This is a picture the New Testament still remembers. Paul writes to the church in Corinth: "Since we have these promises, beloved, let us cleanse ourselves from every defilement of body and spirit, bringing holiness to completion in the fear of God" (2 Cor. 7:1). The apostle John brings us back to it at the very end of the Bible. In Revelation 14:3–4, he reminds us that the redeemed are undefiled and dwell in the presence of the Father and the Lamb. But what of those who are morally defiled? Listen to what he says about the vision of heaven that he sees in Revelation 21:8: "But as for the cowardly, the faithless, the detestable, as for murderers, the sexually immoral, sorcerers, idolaters, and all liars, their portion will be in the lake that burns with fire and sulfur, which is the second death." Those are all moral categories. Now look at what he says at the end of the chapter in verse 27: "But nothing unclean will ever enter it, nor anyone who does what is detestable or false, but only those who are written in the Lamb's book of life." John is talking about defilement and exclusion from glory. But the defilement is moral. The ceremonial pictures of defilement in Leviticus and Numbers point to the dreaded disease of moral defilement, which excludes us eternally—if it is not dealt with—from presence with God. The reason why is that the morally defiled will not dwell in the New Jerusalem. So the law teaches us that God is holy and is going to be treated as holy. He is undefiled. And the defiled cannot besmirch him by dwelling in his presence.

Think of how that principle was applied even to Moses' sister (see Num. 12:1–16; Deut. 24:9). When she was part of a conspiracy to undermine her brother Moses, the mediator whom God had appointed for his people, she contracted leprosy by the judgment of God and was excluded from the camp even though she was a prophetess. Though she had led the people of God in song and praise at the Red Sea, she was excluded from the camp. You see how seriously God takes his holiness: "Miriam, outside the camp. I am holy, you will treat me as holy, and you will treat my mediator as holy. You undermined my mediator? Outside the camp with your leprosy!"

God Is Present—"their camp, in the midst of which I dwell" (5:3)

Yes, these strange commands teach us that God is holy, but they also show us a blessing: God is present. He is present with his people in that camp. Remember that in the Garden of Eden, before the Fall, God was present with Adam and Eve. He walked there among them. And remember what God said to Moses in Exodus 33, after the rebellion of Israel in the false worship of the golden calf. God is so indignant at Israel's idolatry that he says to Moses that he is no longer going to travel with them in their midst. Strikingly, God says, "If for a single moment I should go up among you, I would consume you" (Exod. 33:5).

Essentially God tells Moses, "I'm not going to destroy the children of Israel here because of their idolatry (even though they deserve it), but I am going to send you on to the Promised Land, just without me."

Now unfortunately, if God offered that to most evangelicals, we'd take it. "You can go to heaven, just without communion with me, without my presence." Many of us would take that offer in a heartbeat. Some would even say: "That's a good deal, sign me up."

But not Moses. His response is different: "If your presence will not go with me, do not bring us up from here" (Exod. 33:15). In other words, Moses in effect says: "Lord, if you're not going to be present with us, just go ahead and kill us now. You are the whole reason that we want to go to the Promised Land, because you are better than the Promised Land. You are *the* treasure. Your presence is the whole point. So don't give us any other treasure, even the Promised Land, if you're not also going to give us yourself." Here is the principle: God dwells in the midst of his people. Numbers 5:3 tells us that God dwells in the midst of the camp.

That's the flip side of the laws about excluding defiled people from the camp. The laws remind us that God is there. God is there in the camp. That is a huge blessing and privilege. Yes, his presence requires carefulness about defilement, because he is holy and undefiled, but his presence is the greatest blessing and comfort we could possibly experience. And it is always a marvelous picture of condescending grace.

Do you remember when David purposes to build a temple for God? He is living in a big palace and he says, "Lord, I want to build you a big house" (see 2 Sam. 7:2). And the Lord says, "David, when in all the times of the sojournings of my people have I ever dwelled in a big house? When my people were living in tents in the wilderness do you know where I lived? I lived in a tent right in their midst all the way" (see 2 Sam. 7:5–7). In the camp, God manifests his presence with his people, and therefore, because God is dwelling in the camp, you have to be very careful about defilement. The sacrificial animals have to be taken outside the camp because they are defiled. The refuse of Israel has to be taken outside the camp because it defiles. Because God is present in the camp, those who are ritually defiled because of hemorrhages, discharges, leprosy, or contact with dead bodies have to go outside the camp.

But the positive message in this—the inestimable blessing—is that God dwells with his people, near his people, in the midst of his people. That is our God. He has always been like that. When Jesus comes and tabernacles among us (John 1:14), he simply reflects the heart of his Father, who dwells with and near his people. The comfort of this is incalculable.

God Has Spoken—"as the LORD said to Moses, so the people of Israel did" (5:4)

So these laws teach that God is holy and that God is present. But they also teach that God has spoken. Think of it. Put yourself in this situation. Your son has a discharge of the most ordinary sort. He is fourteen years old, your firstborn, and the priest comes to you and he says, "He's got to go outside the camp. Outside of the safety and protection of the camp in the howling wilderness of Sinai." And that deeply concerned father who loves his son as his pride and joy, nevertheless, as a humble and Bible-obeying Hebrew believer, says, "Because that's what God has said, we'll obey. Son, you'll be alright, we'll obey. The Lord will protect you outside of the camp."

Or, imagine that your wife has contracted a skin disease and the priest comes and says, "That woman whom you love more than life itself, she's got to go outside the camp." And every molecule of your being screams out, "Not her! Send me outside the camp, but not her!" Listen to the language of Numbers 5:4: "The people of Israel did so, and put them outside the camp; as the LORD said to Moses, so the people of Israel did."

Would you have obeyed the word of God like they did? If it was your son or daughter, your husband or wife, your best friend?

This is what it means to live by the Book. It's when we go to this Book and it tells us to do things that cost us, things we don't want to do, even things that may break our hearts, then, *then*, we find out if we really love and trust God, and believe his word. It is in those moments when we are called to follow the Book when it's hard, that our hearts' true natures are revealed. You do what you believe. And you won't obey what you don't believe.

There are all sorts of people who want to call themselves "people of the Book," and when they find things in it that make them out of step with this culture, or their desires, what do they do? They reinterpret the Book. Yes, in those places where this Book says things that butt up against our will or our desires, we're tempted to reinterpret it.

There are people right now in our time and culture, people who claim to be Christians, trying to do this with the Bible's crystal-clear teaching on sexual ethics. Same-sex marriage and same-sex sexual activity is forbidden in the Bible, and yet people try to rationalize their own desires and behavior by changing their interpretation of the Book. But let me be clear: not one of us is immune from the temptation to change the meaning of God's Word to make it less demanding, less intrusive—all in the pursuit of giving ourselves an excuse to do what we want to do.

There are many idolatries—Calvin said our hearts are idol factories—and the question is, "Are we going to bow the knee to God and live under the Book because God has spoken, believing and obeying every word commanded to us, or are we going to make it up as we go along?" And if we do what we want rather than what God commands, then we are not like the faithful children of Israel who sent their loved ones out in obedience to the spoken word of God, just as the Lord commanded them.

These laws provided a test of faith. Do we really believe God has spoken, even when what he has spoken seems hard and is hard? Moses tells us here that, in this instance, the people in the wilderness showed they believed the Lord had spoken, by obeying his commands.

So these seemingly strange laws are profoundly theological. They teach us that God is holy, God is present, and God has spoken.

I also want you to see how encompassing this law is. You really need to look at Leviticus 13—15 to see the comprehensiveness of it. Leviticus 15:1–12 will give you a sense of the demands of the law of discharges:

> The LORD spoke to Moses and Aaron, saying, "Speak to the people of Israel and say to them, When any man has a discharge from his body, his discharge is unclean. And this is the law of his uncleanness for a discharge: whether his body runs with his discharge, or his body is blocked up by his discharge, it is his uncleanness. Every bed on which the one with the discharge lies shall be unclean, and everything on which he sits shall be unclean. And anyone who touches his bed shall wash his clothes and bathe himself in water and be unclean until the evening. And whoever sits on anything on which the one with the discharge has sat shall wash his clothes and bathe himself in water and be unclean until the evening. And whoever touches the body of the one with the discharge shall wash his clothes and bathe himself in water and be unclean until the evening. And if the one with the discharge spits on someone who is clean, then he shall wash his clothes and bathe himself in water and be unclean until the evening. And any saddle on which the one with the discharge rides shall be unclean. And whoever touches anything that was under him shall be unclean until the evening. And whoever carries such things shall wash his clothes and bathe himself in water and be unclean until the evening. Anyone whom the one

with the discharge touches without having rinsed his
hands in water shall wash his clothes and bathe himself
in water and be unclean until the evening. And an earth-
enware vessel that the one with the discharge touches
shall be broken, and every vessel of wood shall be rinsed
in water."

Did you see the expansion of Numbers 5:1–4 here? Not only
is the one with the skin disease or discharge unclean or defiled,
anyone who comes into contact with him is defiled or unclean.
This uncleanness is contagious! If you come into contact with it,
you're unclean. That is how comprehensive these commands are
about defilement. They convey a moral lesson. They say, "You are a
defiled sinner, everything you touch is unclean, and everyone who
touches you or what you have touched is unclean."

The Christological Purpose of the Laws in Numbers

Now, we have argued that these laws were given for a practical
purpose and a theological purpose, but, ultimately, they serve a
Christological purpose. They point us to Jesus Christ. How?

Well, do you remember Luke telling us about Jesus' walk
on the road to Emmaus with two disconsolate disciples (Luke
24:13–35)? As an answer to their crisis of faith, Jesus gives them a
systematic Christological study of the Old Testament Scriptures.
Luke tells us that he said to them:

"O foolish ones, and slow of heart to believe all that
the prophets have spoken! Was it not necessary that
the Christ should suffer these things and enter into his
glory?" And beginning with Moses and all the Prophets,

he interpreted to them in all the Scriptures the things
concerning himself. (Luke 24:25–27)

Beginning with Moses (the Torah, the Pentateuch) and all
the Prophets (the rest of the Old Testament), Jesus explained how
the Scriptures point to his person and work, to his humiliation
and exaltation! Well, what if I told you that that same Luke who
recorded that amazing conversation, also knows our passage in
Numbers 5:1–4? And, in canonical order, in Luke 5 and Luke 8,
he takes us to an encounter between Jesus and a leper, Jesus and
a woman with a discharge, and Jesus and a little dead girl.

Luke tells us of Jesus' encounter with a leper in Luke 5:12–13:

While he was in one of the cities, there came a man full
of leprosy. And when he saw Jesus, he fell on his face
and begged him, "Lord, if you will, you can make me
clean." And Jesus stretched out his hand and touched
him, saying, "I will; be clean." And immediately the leprosy left him.

Take the force of this in—what Luke, the physician, tells
you. Jesus stretches out his hand and *touches* the leper! Every
good Hebrew there is screaming, "Jesus, don't touch him! You will
become unclean!" But Jesus "stretched out his hand and touched
him, saying, 'I will; be clean.' And immediately the leprosy left
him."

Jesus touches the unclean man and something amazing happens: Jesus doesn't become unclean, but the man becomes clean.
Luke is telling you that Jesus can do what the ceremonial law
couldn't do. You can read all the way through Leviticus and do you
know what it doesn't tell you? It doesn't tell you how to heal a leper.
It doesn't tell you how to make an unclean, defiled leper *clean*. It
tells you what to do if a person becomes clean, but it doesn't tell
you how to make anybody clean. The priest isn't given a solution

about how to make somebody clean, because there is nobody that can make someone clean but Jesus. Jesus touches that leprous man and he makes him clean!

Then, as Jesus is about to minister to a worried father and a fretting family who are fearing for their daughter's life, he encounters a woman with a discharge in Luke 8:40–56.

> Now when Jesus returned, the crowd welcomed him,
> for they were all waiting for him. And there came a man
> named Jairus, who was a ruler of the synagogue. And
> falling at Jesus' feet, he implored him to come to his
> house, for he had an only daughter, about twelve years of
> age, and she was dying.
>
>   As Jesus went, the people pressed around him. And
> there was a woman who had had a discharge of blood
> for twelve years, and though she had spent all her living
> on physicians, she could not be healed by anyone. She
> came up behind him and touched the fringe of his gar-
> ment. . . . (vv. 40–44)

Once again, every faithful, ceremonial-law-keeping Hebrew there, had they seen it and understood her condition, would have screamed out to Jesus, "Don't let her touch you!" But she does touch him and she becomes clean. He does not become unclean. Luke writes, "And immediately her discharge of blood ceased" (v. 44).

Why? Because Jesus can do what the ceremonial law can't do. He can make her clean.

> And Jesus said, "Who was it that touched me?" When all
> denied it, Peter said, "Master, the crowds surround you
> and are pressing in on you!" But Jesus said, "Someone
> touched me, for I perceive that power has gone out from
> me." And when the woman saw that she was not hid-
> den, she came trembling, and falling down before him

declared in the presence of all the people why she had touched him, and how she had been immediately healed. And he said to her, "Daughter, your faith has made you well; go in peace." (vv. 45–48)

Then, in the wake of the unmitigated joy that this daughter of Israel must have been experiencing after her deliverance from an affliction that had vexed her for a dozen years, crushing news comes to the father he was on his way to help.

And now, Jesus is faced with something beyond any priest or teacher. He's faced with the ultimate defilement. Death. Surely there was nothing that could be done.

While he was still speaking, someone from the ruler's house came and said, "Your daughter is dead; do not trouble the Teacher any more." But Jesus on hearing this answered him, "Do not fear; only believe, and she will be well." And when he came to the house, he allowed no one to enter with him, except Peter and John and James, and the father and mother of the child. And all were weeping and mourning for her, but he said, "Do not weep, for she is not dead but sleeping." And they laughed at him, knowing that she was dead. But taking her by the hand . . . (vv. 49–54)

Again, Jesus touches the corpse of the little girl. And every observant Jew would have screamed out: "No, Jesus, don't touch that dead body! You'll become unclean!"

Taking her by the hand he called, saying, "Child, arise." And her spirit returned, and she got up at once. And he directed that something should be given her to eat. And her parents were amazed, but he charged them to tell no one what had happened. (vv. 54–56)

He touches her, he doesn't become unclean, and she lives! He speaks to her like a Hebrew father would address a little child when it's time to get up in the morning. "Sweet girl, get up." "My child, wake up." And. She. Lives.

Who is this? Who is this that can touch the unclean and defiled and not become unclean and defiled? Who is this who can touch the unclean and defiled and make them clean and undefiled? Who is this who can touch the dead and speak them to life? Luke has a megaphone up to your heart and he's proclaiming, "This is a mediator who can do things that Moses couldn't do, that the priests couldn't do, that even the high priest couldn't do. He can touch lepers—and he's not unclean, but they're made clean. He can touch people with discharges—and he's not unclean, but they're made clean. He can touch dead people—and they come to life. Who is this? This is the Son of God made flesh! This is the only mediator for all God's people, "who forgives all your iniquity, who heals all your diseases, who redeems your life from the pit, who crowns you with steadfast love and mercy" (Ps. 103:3–4).

Why all this about defilement and Numbers 5? Luke knows that only Jesus can address the defilement and uncleanness, both ritual and actual, that Numbers 5:1–4 points to. And brother pastors, you need to know that too.

Jesus Knows What to Do

If you're going to point people to Jesus, then you need to know that Jesus knows what to do with them when you bring them to him. When the weight of the sense of our own defilement finally comes home, when we meet our true selves in all our uncleanness in the middle of the night, what do we say in our hearts?

Or, when your people say things like, "You don't know what kind of life I've lived. You don't know what I've done. I don't think anyone can forgive me of my sin, certainly not THAT one."

Or, when that sense of the holiness of God and the sinfulness of man comes upon our hearts, what do we say? Do we say, "I don't think there's any way my defilement can be dealt with"?

Not at all, because it's in that moment we need to know that our Jesus knows how to deal with our defilement. And what does he do? He reaches right out for that defilement. And, like Luke's God-fearing Jews, we scream out in our heart: *Lord, you don't know what I've done. Don't touch that defilement. It is my shame; I don't want anybody to know that I've done THAT. I don't even think that God can forgive me of THAT. Jesus, don't reach out and touch that defilement. You'll become unclean!*

And what does he do? He reaches right out and touches that defilement—and he doesn't become unclean, but you become clean.

Brothers, when you take people to Jesus, he knows what to do with them. There is power in him to deal with our defilement:

"What can wash away my sin?
Nothing but the blood of Jesus."

How Jesus Makes Us Clean

This brings me to where I want us to go. Because this is not the end of the New Testament's references to the realities of Numbers 5. Let's turn to Hebrews 13, and as we do, let's ask ourselves, "How is it that Jesus does this? Exactly how is it that Jesus touches the defiled and he's not defiled and they are made undefiled? How is it that he touches someone who is unclean and they are made clean and he's not made unclean? How is it that he is able to grant this forgiveness and pardon and cleansing?"

Hebrews 13:10–13 helps us with the answer:

We have an altar from which those who serve the tent
have no right to eat. For the bodies of those animals
whose blood is brought into the holy places by the high
priest as a sacrifice for sin are burned outside the camp.
So Jesus also suffered outside the gate in order to sanc-
tify the people through his own blood. Therefore let us
go to him outside the camp and bear the reproach he
endured.

Do you see what's going on here? How is it that Jesus touches
the unclean? How can the undefiled, sinless Son of God touch
the unclean and make them clean? Because he says to his Father,
"Father, I want to bear their reproach in their place outside the
camp."

Do you see what is going on in that "outside the camp" picture? To be "outside the camp" is to be cut off from the presence
of God. That is what defilement deserves. Think for a moment
of the Aaronic blessing: "The LORD bless you and keep you; the
LORD make his face to shine upon you and be gracious to you;
the LORD lift up his countenance upon you and give you peace"
(Num. 6:24–26). With this in mind, Jesus says to his loving Father,
"Father, I know that in your great love for your people and in your
infinite holiness and righteous perfection, the only way your grace
and favor can be righteously pronounced on your people—the
only way the Aaronic benediction can be righteously pronounced
on your people—is if someone bears their reproach, bears their
shame, bears their guilt, bears their uncleanness, and bears their
defilement. Father, I want to do that for them. I want to do that for
them because I love them, just like you love them, and because I
want to glorify you in bringing them home to you, back into your
holy presence. So I will go 'outside the camp.' I will be cut off so

that they will not be cut off. I want to bear their reproach so that they can be clean."

And so, the sinless, undefiled Son of God hears not, "The LORD bless you and keep you," but "the LORD curse you and cut you off" so that you can hear, "The LORD bless you and keep you."

The sinless, undefiled Son of God hears not, "The LORD lift up his countenance upon you and be gracious to you," but "I will turn my face away from you and show you no mercy, but only the just judgment due defiled sinners."

The sinless, undefiled Son of God hears not, "The LORD make his face to shine upon you and give you peace," but "my face will look on you in righteous indignation and you will bear my wrath and have no peace; you will be cut off from your people, driven away from the comfortable presence of your God and it's enjoyment."

And in bearing their reproach, their defilement, they will be made clean, whiter than snow.

That is what Jesus does.

So, when you share the gospel with non-Christians and they object, "You don't understand; you don't know who I am and what I am like and what I've done," you can say, "Friend, there is nothing, absolutely nothing, that he can't touch and clean in you. Nothing. There is no disease that he can't fix in your soul because he has borne the unmitigated wrath of God in your place outside the camp so that you can dwell in the presence of God, in him, by faith, forever."

Second Corinthians 5:21 tells us, "He made him to be sin who knew no sin, so that in him we might become the righteousness of God."

There's the motivation for evangelism! Don't you want to tell everybody in the world about Jesus? And where does the author of Hebrews take you? Let us respond and say ourselves, "He went outside the camp for me? I want to go outside the camp. I want to go to lepers, and I want to go to people with discharges. And I want to go to people who are dead in trespasses and sins, and I want to tell them about the one man who can do something about their sin, the one man who can save their lives: the Lord Jesus Christ. I want to share the gospel!" Go!

CHAPTER 8

Pleading and Predestination
(Romans 9)

John Piper

The ninth chapter of Romans is the fullest, most forth-right, and blunt chapter on the freedom and sovereignty of God in all the Bible. It contains statements like:

For I could wish that I myself were accursed and cut off from Christ for the sake of my brothers, my kinsmen according to the flesh. (v. 3)

Not all who are descended from Israel belong to Israel. (v. 6)

And not only so, but also when Rebekah had conceived children by one man, our forefather Isaac, though they were not yet born and had done nothing either good or bad—in order that God's purpose of election might continue, not because of works but because of him who calls—she was told, "The older will serve the younger." (vv. 10–12)

"Jacob I loved, but Esau I hated." (v. 13)

"I will have mercy on whom I have mercy, and I will have compassion on whom I have compassion." (v. 15)

"It depends not on him who wills or him who runs, but on God who has mercy." (v. 16 NASB)

"For this very purpose I have raised you up, that I might show my power in you, and that my name might be proclaimed in all the earth." (v. 17)

"He has mercy on whomever he wills, and he hardens whomever he wills." (v. 18)

"Why does he still find fault? . . . Who are you, O man, to answer back to God?" (vv. 19–20)

Most people who read Romans 9 are shocked. Very few are so steeped in the biblical spirit of the majesty and freedom of God, that these words make sense. And there is a long line of scholarly effort to nullify the true implications of this chapter—claiming that it has nothing to do with individuals and nothing to do with eternal destinies, but has only to do with corporate peoples and historical roles. That will not stand scrutiny, as we will see shortly.

Why Is Romans 9 Here?

My main questions are: Why is this here? Why did Paul even feel compelled to lead us into these things? I assume that this is holy Scripture—that it is inspired and infallible and, as Paul would say, "profitable for teaching, for reproof, for correction, and for training in righteousness, that the man of God may be complete, equipped for every good work" (2 Tim. 3:16–17). Including the work of personal evangelism and world missions.

I assume that these words are here not to undermine but to strengthen our evangelism. I assume they are here to empower, and deepen, and stabilize, and advance, and make more fruitful the cause of world missions, and the cause of neighborhood evangelism. I assume that if the reality of Romans 9 were rightly understood and rightly felt, more people will be brought into the kingdom with white-hot affection for God than if this were not in the Bible.

So I ask again my main questions: Why is this here? Why did Paul feel compelled to lead us into these things at this point in the argument of Romans?

And once we've answered that, we will ask: And how does this answer affect Paul's relationship with lost people? How does it affect his evangelism? And the three answers we will focus on are these:

1. In Romans 9:2, it sustains him in the "great sorrow and unceasing anguish" of his heart for the lost.
2. In Romans 11:13–14 it empowers his labors to persuade the lost to be believe and be saved.
3. In Romans 10:1 it impels the earnestness of his prayer for the salvation of his kinsmen.

So let's turn to the main question: Why is Romans 9, with these weighty teachings about the sovereignty of God in salvation, brought in to the argument of Romans just at this point?

Paul has just come to the end of the most magnificent eight chapters in the Bible. They reach a crescendo in Romans 8 with the most spectacular promises about our standing and our security in Christ with God forever. Here are some of the truths Paul tells us in Romans 8:

"There is . . . no condemnation for those who are in Christ Jesus." (v. 1)

"If the Spirit of him who raised Jesus from the dead dwells in you, he who raised Christ Jesus from the dead will also give life to your mortal bodies." (v. 11)

"We are children of God, and if children, then heirs— heirs of God and fellow heirs with Christ." (vv. 16–17)

"The sufferings of this present time are not worth comparing with the glory that is to be revealed to us." (v. 18)

"The creation will be set free from its bondage to corruption and obtain the freedom of the glory of the children of God." (v. 21)

"For those who love God all things work together for good." (v. 28)

"Those whom he predestined he also called, and those whom he called he also justified, and those whom he justified he also glorified." (v. 30)

"If God is for us, who can be against us?" (v. 31)

"He who did not spare his own Son but gave him up for us all, how will he not also with him graciously give us all things?" (v. 32)

"Who shall bring any charge against God's elect?" (v. 33)

"Who shall separate us from the love of Christ?" (v. 35)

"Neither death nor life, nor angels nor rulers, nor things present nor things to come, nor powers, nor height nor depth, nor anything else in all creation, will be able to separate us from the love of God in Christ Jesus our Lord." (vv. 38–39)

The God of Israel has embraced the world. He has sent his Son, inaugurated a new covenant, set in motion a global mission to rescue sinners, and promised a glorious consummation for the universe and for the children of God.

And all of this is totally dependent on the faithfulness of God, the integrity of God, and the promise-keeping righteousness of God. If God does not keep his word, all of Romans 8, and all of salvation history, fall to the ground. And with it all our hope—every practical benefit, every sweet experience of the gospel fails, if the word of God fails.

And as Paul turns to Romans 9 that horrible possibility is precisely what he is dealing with. Israel, the chosen people of God, with untold privileges and blessings and promises from God, has rejected her Messiah. The kingdom has been taken away from them (Matt. 21:43). Gentiles are streaming in "from east and west [to] recline at table with Abraham, Isaac, and Jacob in the kingdom of heaven, while the sons of the kingdom will be thrown into the outer darkness" (Matt. 8:11–12). So it seems that the promises to Israel have failed. God has not kept his word. His word has fallen. He was not faithful to his covenant. That's what Paul is dealing with in Romans 9—indeed all of Romans 9—11.

Look with me at verses 1–3:

> I am speaking the truth in Christ—I am not lying; my
> conscience bears me witness in the Holy Spirit—that I
> have great sorrow and unceasing anguish in my heart.
> For I could wish that I myself were accursed and cut off
> from Christ for the sake of my brothers, my kinsmen
> according to the flesh.

Paul lives with sorrow and anguish over the fact that his Jewish kinsmen, for the most part, have rejected the Messiah and are accursed—anathema—and cut off from the Redeemer. That's clear in verse 3: "I could wish that I myself were accursed and cut off from Christ for the sake of my brothers." Paul stands ready, were it possible, to be damned for them. But God will not damn someone for loving others so much that he is willing to be damned. So he is not damned. They are. Cursed—anathema—cut off from Christ.

Not all of them, of course. He himself is a Jew, as he is very aware, and he will make much of in chapter 11. But as a whole, the Jewish people turned away from the Messiah and are therefore accursed and cut off from the Savior. And this is true in spite of the spectacular benefits that belong to the Jewish people. Paul writes in Romans 9:4–5:

> They are Israelites, and to them belong the adoption, the
> glory, the covenants, the giving of the law, the worship,
> and the promises. To them belong the patriarchs, and
> from their race, according to the flesh, is the Christ, who
> is God over all, blessed forever. Amen.

In spite of all that, they are eternally lost.

What can this mean but that God has failed his people? God is not faithful. His word of promise is not sure. We know this is the issue as Paul sees it, because of what he says next in verse 6: "But it is not as though the word of God has failed." He preempts the objection. No, he says. That is not what has happened. But the fact that he must say this shows that this is what some were saying: If God's covenant people are perishing as a whole, then what good are all these covenant promises? And if these covenant promises to Israel are this uncertain, what becomes of all these promises in Romans 8? What good are all the gospel promises to the people of the new covenant?

The Question of Romans 9: Is God Trustworthy?

That's the issue in Romans 9. Is God faithful? Is he trustworthy? Does he keep his promises? And the issue is not one of mere corporate peoples and their historical roles. The issue, that stands out with shocking vividness in verse 3 is that vast numbers of individual Israelites—particular kinsmen of Paul—are perishing. They are accursed. They are cut off from the Messiah, the Savior. And Paul has great sorrow and unceasing anguish over their doom.

That is the issue. Has God's word failed in view of that? And the reason this issue is pressing just at this point in Romans is that, if the word of God falls then all of Romans 8 falls—and all our hopes with it.

To answer this objection, Paul takes us into the deepest counsels of God concerning election and predestination. So the answer to my main questions as to why Romans 9 is here, and why Paul would lead us into these weighty matters, is that Paul believes we need to know the deepest foundation of God's faithfulness in relation to who is saved and who is accursed. We need to know the deepest roots of his promise-keeping faithfulness.

The depths of Romans 9 exist just here to provide an unshakable foundation for the heights of Romans 8. Paul takes us into the doctrine of unconditional election and predestination because it answers the destabilizing questions about the faithfulness of God in the failure of Israel. Or, to say it more generally, Paul takes us into unconditional election as the deepest foundation for our assurance that nothing can thwart his saving purpose, and therefore nothing can compromise his faithfulness, and therefore nothing can undermine his word of promise, and therefore all of Romans 8 stands.

Three Reasons God's Word Still Stands

Now how does Paul show this?

His argument has three levels. First, the word of God has not fallen because the covenant promises were never intended to be valid for every ethnic Israelite, but only the true Israel. Second, the true Israel are brought into being not by human means but by God's word of promise. Third, before that the true Israel were chosen by God unconditionally. The upshot of these three levels of argument is that the word of God's promise will never fail, the security of the children of God rests ultimately not in anything they do or are, but in God who has mercy.

Not All Israel Is "True Israel"

Consider level one of this argument.

In Romans 9:6–8 Paul states the same premise three times in different words, namely, that the word of God's promise has not fallen because the covenant promises were never intended to be valid for every ethnic Israelite, but only the true Israel. First, in verse 6: "It is not as though the word of God has failed. For not all who are descended from Israel belong to Israel." There is Israel, and then there is Israel, Paul says. There are the physical descendants, and then there is Israel—it seems suitable to call it "true Israel."

So what's the point? The point is that the word of promise has not fallen because it did not apply to all the ethnic descendants, but to the true Israel. It does not apply to those who are accursed and cut off from Christ (v. 3).

In verse 7 he says it again: "And not all are children of Abraham because they are his offspring." There are physical offspring and there are children. And being a physical offspring doesn't make you a "true child."

Finally, he says it again in verse 8: "It is not the children of the flesh who are the children of God, but the children of the promise are counted as offspring." There are children of the flesh. And there are children of God. And they do not correspond. They are not identical.

So the first level of Paul's answer to the charge that the word of God has fallen, is to say: No, the promise was never intended to apply to every ethnic Israelite. It was made to the true Israel (v. 6), the true children of Abraham (v. 7), the children of God, the true children of promise (v. 8). The word of God has not fallen. It stands unshakable for the true Israel.

True Israel Is of God, Not Man

The second level of Paul's argument is to show that this true Israel is brought into being not by human means but by God's word of promise. At the end of verse 7 Paul cites Genesis 21:12 where God says to Abraham, "Through Isaac shall your offspring be named." Abraham wanted Ishmael to be the heir of promise. He had taken matters into his own hands and produced an heir.

Ishmael represents a child of the flesh, not a child of promise. A child that human means can bring about. Not a miracle child. Not a child produced by the sovereign word of God. So God says No. He will not be the heir. "Through Isaac shall your offspring be named."

And then in verse 9 Paul cites Genesis 18:10 and shows how the promise works: "For this is what the promise said: 'About this time next year I will return, and Sarah shall have a son.'" Sarah is barren. Sarah is ninety years old. Sarah cannot produce an heir. And that's the point. God's "word of promise" brings about the child. This is what it means to be a "child of promise," a "child of God," a true Israelite whose status as an heir is not owing to anything man can do, but only what God can do.

So the word of God has not fallen, first because the covenant promises were never intended to be valid for every ethnic Israelite, but only the true Israel. Second, God's word has not fallen because true Israel are brought into being not by everything so vulnerable and uncertain as human means but by God's word of promise. This word is not so fragile as to depend on man-created children of the flesh. It stands as absolutely sure because it creates what it promises. Ishmael illustrates what can be brought into being by human ability. Isaac illustrates what is brought into being by divine sovereignty.

True Israel Was Chosen Unconditionally

Which brings us now to level three in Paul's argument, namely, this true Israel—these promise-created children of God—were chosen as heirs unconditionally.

Paul moves from the illustration of Isaac and Ishmael to the illustration of Jacob and Esau. Four things make Jacob and Esau a striking illustration of the point Paul wants to make. His point here is not the supernatural origin of the children of God. That was illustrated with Isaac, not here. The point here is the utter freedom of God in choosing the children of promise uncondition-ally. And for that, Jacob and Esau are a better illustration than Isaac and Ishmael.

First, they were twins in the same womb, but Isaac was born thirteen years after Ishmael. Second, Jacob and Esau had the same parents, while Ishmael had a Gentile mother. Third, God chose the heir before they were born or had done good or bad while God had thirteen years to watch Ishmael's behavior. Fourth, against all convention and precedent, God chose the younger to be the heir, not the elder.

Why did God do it this way? Paul gives a vivid statement of the answer in verses 11–12: "Though they were not yet born and had done nothing either good or bad—in order that God's purpose of election might continue, not because of works but because of him who calls—she was told, 'The older will serve the younger.'"

There's the word *election*. Election has been lying just beneath the surface from verse 6 on: God chose a true Israel (v. 6). God chose the true children of Abraham (v. 7). God created the chil-dren of promise, the children of God (v. 8). And now it is explicit. God was doing all this, all the way along, at every stage in the his-tory of Israel, so that "his purpose of election might continue, not because of works but because of him who calls."

Notice: almost everywhere else in Paul where "not because of works" is contrasted with something, the contrast is faith. Not because of works but because of faith. But not here. Because that is absolutely not the point. The point is: in the womb they had done nothing good or evil. They had not believed or disbelieved. They had not produced any conditions at all. That's the point. This was unconditional. The only decisive cause in this affair was God—"not because of works but because of him who calls."

Which is why Paul underscores the point three more times:

Verse 15: "I will have mercy on whom I have mercy."

Verse 16: "So then it depends not on human will or exertion, but on God, who has mercy."

Verse 18: "So then he has mercy on whomever he wills, and he hardens whomever he wills."

So the answer to our main question is: Paul leads us into the doctrine of unconditional election at this point to show us that the word of God to Israel has not fallen. God's word of promise from the beginning has infallibly created a people for himself. This true Israel—the children of promise, the children of God—were chosen unconditionally, and therefore the saving promise of God for them cannot fail, because ultimately, decisively, it does not depend on them—at all. Therefore, fear not, all you new covenant children of God, that security, that assurance, that confidence is what the doctrine of unconditional election is for. And because of that, it is precious beyond words. The promises of Romans 8 stand forever.

How Does Election Affect Evangelism?

How does this reality affect Paul's relationship with lost people? How does it affect his evangelism? How should it affect ours? Three brief observations.

1. It should destroy superiority and promote great sorrow for the lost.

This reality sustains him in the "great sorrow and unceasing anguish" of his heart for his kinsmen. Paul writes in 9:1–2, "I am speaking the truth in Christ—I am not lying; my conscience bears me witness in the Holy Spirit—that I have great sorrow and unceasing anguish in my heart."

When Paul looks on a sea of Jewish faces, all of them drowning in an ocean of unbelief, and he remembers himself snatched, by an invisible hand, out of that sea, and gasping helplessly for breath in the house of Judas in Damascus, and a man named Ananias opening his eyes; and when he asks, "Why me?" there is no answer but this: It is a "gift of God's grace" (Eph. 3:7); "[You are] a chosen instrument of mine to carry my name before the Gentiles" (Acts 9:15). When Paul pondered this, the effect it had was to make him feel great sorrow and ceaseless anguish for his kinsmen who were still perishing in the sea of unbelief, where he deserved to be.

The doctrine of unconditional election destroys every sense of superiority. It leaves us weeping with the sheer wonder of thankfulness, and this weeping flows over into great sorrow for the lost. If we don't feel this, the problem is not that we believe in unconditional election, but that the truth of it has not been believed and therefore has not broken us.

2. It should empower our labors to persuade the lost to believe and be saved.

Paul writes later in Romans 11:13–14, "Inasmuch then as I am an apostle to the Gentiles, I magnify my ministry in order somehow to make my fellow Jews jealous, and thus save some of them." Paul knows that the sovereign, electing God, uses human means. God tells Paul that he is his elect instrument (Acts 9:15), his chosen means. And so are we.

This is how God saves his elect. He uses planning, preaching, writing, loving, caring, pursing, pleading people. Again, he writes in 11:14: "In order somehow I might make my fellow Jews jealous" of the Gentile enjoyment of *their* inheritance. "Somehow!" Here's

Paul the evangelistic strategist: Somehow! Somehow! I must find a way. O, grant me to find a way to awaken desire in the lost!

The next time you are sitting across the table from an unbeliever who is willing to listen, tell him the gospel, and then plead with him. "God [is] making his appeal through [me. I] implore you on behalf of Christ, be reconciled to God" (2 Cor. 5:20). He may have never heard anybody say: "I want you." God said that to you, before you were born or had done anything to deserve it.

3. The doctrine of unconditional election impels the earnestness of Paul's prayer for the salvation of his kinsmen.

He writes in Romans 10:1, "Brothers, my heart's desire and prayer to God for them is that they may be saved." Don't miss this: his heart is aching and his prayers are rising. Again: "My heart's desire and prayer to God for them is that they may be saved." Not only do we persuade and plead, but we pray. God saves his elect through the prayers of his elect.

Jesus Is Calling

Let me close with a real illustration that moved me deeply in this matter of pleading and praying.

My father was an evangelist—a faithful and fruitful herald of the gospel of grace for over sixty years. In his old traditional way he would give invitations at the end of every meeting, every night. One of the songs he used over and over was "Softly and Tenderly." The lyrics were simple:

> *Softly and tenderly Jesus is calling,*
> *Calling for you and for me;*
> *See, on the portals He's waiting and watching,*
> *Watching for you and for me.*

Come home, come home,
You who are weary, come home;
Earnestly, tenderly, Jesus is calling,
Calling, O sinner, come home!

Can a lover of unconditional election use that song? Is Jesus just waiting and watching for sinners to come home? The song doesn't say he is just waiting and watching.

Picture my father. He is now standing on the floor not in the pulpit. There are about three hundred people in the room. He had just preached a glorious message of gospel truth. Now he's looking the people in the eye, "Would you come? Come to Jesus, he will have you. He will not reject you. Come."

And then picture him saying between the verses of the song, "Every head bowed. Every eye closed. Every saint praying." And back about ten pews there is a mother standing beside her college-age son who is a hardened, angry unbeliever. She asked him to come, and to make her happy he came. And now every saint is praying. What is she praying?

She is praying, "O God, please, in the name of Jesus, pour out your Holy Spirit. Open the blind eyes of my son. Take out his heart of stone and give him a heart of flesh. Grant him to see this waiting, watching Jesus as true and beautiful and irresistibly compelling. Overcome his rebellion. Save him, O sovereign God." And as she prays, her son moves past her and walks to the front and collapses into the arms of my father, and into the arms of Jesus.

And God Almighty—through his own unconditional election, and through the crucified, risen, waiting, watching Christ, and through our tears and preaching and pleading and praying, and through the all-conquering Holy Spirit—saves sinners.

CHAPTER 9

Praying and Providence
(Exodus 32—33)

David Platt

✝ "Prayer is a huge hole in the canvas of the reformed resurgence—and most other forms of Christianity today."

These words were spoken to me by John Piper in a recent conversation concerning current trends in the church landscape. By God's grace, we have witnessed a revival of theology focused on the sovereignty of God, the sinfulness of man, and the wonder of the gospel. By God's grace, we have seen a renewed interest in ecclesiology and the marks of the church that matter most to God. By God's grace, we are watching the ways that this theology and ecclesiology fuel and inform missiology, as zeal for God's glory propels church planters into cities and compels missionaries to move overseas. A plethora of books written and blogs posted;

conferences held; and conversations on theology, ecclesiology, and missiology all attest to the prevalence of these trends.

Yet, in the midst of it all, something glaring is missing—"a huge hole" in Piper's words. And that hole is prayer. D. A. Carson similarly laments "the sheer prayerlessness that characterizes so much of the Western church."[36]

A Totally Foreign Concept

Where are the plethora of books written and blogs posted, conversations had and conferences held on prayer and fasting in our day? We look back at the days of the Westminster Assembly when brothers gathered together not just for preaching, but also for praying. They would preach for an hour, then pray for an hour; they would pray for two hours, then preach for two hours. Such a concept is totally foreign among us today. Amid a right emphasis on the preaching of God's Word, where is the equally right emphasis on prayer as God's people? Why is it that we spend hours every week in the church devoted to the ministry of the Word, while we spend minutes every week in the church devoted to the ministry of prayer?

Look at mighty movements of God from biblical and contemporary history, from Nehemiah to the New Testament church, from seventeenth-century Puritans to nineteenth-century laymen and students, and you will see a steady stream of men and women who were known for their passionate panting after God. They were known for their desperate desire to love him, to belong with him, and to experience power with him from the confines of the prayer closet to the corners of planet earth. I fear that this is not what we are known for in our day.

We are known today for our preaching and our teaching, our writing and our blogging, our organizing and our strategizing, our planning and our planting. But we are not known for our praying and our fasting, and in this, we are in profound danger of missing the whole point. God wills for us to be a praying people. God wills to work in the world in ways that echo the cries of his children. Maybe another way to put that would be: God brings about remarkable change in the world in response to the prayers of his people. Or, just to be clear, we could say: Our prayers affect the way God acts in the world.

Now I know that as soon as I say that, I make many of us uncomfortable. *Our* prayers affect the way *God* acts in the world? Am I sure about that? What about God's sovereignty and God's providence? Can our prayers really affect what God has already predestined to occur? The very question that causes us to wonder how much prayer can accomplish shows that we have a defective understanding of divine providence.

My aim is to show with the Word of God how a right doctrine of providence results in relentless devotion to prayer. Moreover, I aim to show how a right doctrine of providence leads to relentless confidence in prayer and relentless power through prayer. In order to show us this, I want to look at one of the most biblically baffling, practically provoking stories in all of Scripture, which begins in Exodus 32. After God miraculously rescues his people out of slavery in Egypt, he leads them to Mount Sinai, where he reveals his glory to them and gives them his law. Moses goes up on the mountain to meet with God while the people wait at the foot of the mountain. As the people's representative stands at the top of the mountain with God on their behalf, this is what happens:

> When the people saw that Moses delayed to come down
> from the mountain, the people gathered themselves
> together to Aaron and said to him, "Up, make us gods
> who shall go before us. As for this Moses, the man who

brought us up out of the land of Egypt, we do not know what has become of him." So Aaron said to them, "Take off the rings of gold that are in the ears of your wives, your sons, and your daughters, and bring them to me." So all the people took off the rings of gold that were in their ears and brought them to Aaron. And he received the gold from their hand and fashioned it with a graving tool and made a golden calf. And they said, "These are your gods, O Israel, who brought you up out of the land of Egypt!" When Aaron saw this, he built an altar before it. And Aaron made a proclamation and said, "Tomorrow shall be a feast to the LORD." And they rose up early the next day and offered burnt offerings and brought peace offerings. And the people sat down to eat and drink and rose up to play.

And the LORD said to Moses, "Go down, for your people, whom you brought up out of the land of Egypt, have corrupted themselves. They have turned aside quickly out of the way that I commanded them. They have made for themselves a golden calf and have worshiped it and sacrificed to it and said, 'These are your gods, O Israel, who brought you up out of the land of Egypt!'" And the LORD said to Moses, "I have seen this people, and behold, it is a stiff-necked people. Now therefore let me alone, that my wrath may burn hot against them and I may consume them, in order that I may make a great nation of you."

But Moses implored the LORD his God and said, "O LORD, why does your wrath burn hot against your people, whom you have brought out of the land of Egypt with great power and with a mighty hand? Why should the Egyptians say, 'With evil intent did he bring them out, to

kill them in the mountains and to consume them from
the face of the earth'? Turn from your burning anger and
relent from this disaster against your people. Remember
Abraham, Isaac, and Israel, your servants, to whom you
swore by your own self, and said to them, 'I will multiply
your offspring as the stars of heaven, and all this land
that I have promised I will give to your offspring, and
they shall inherit it forever.'" And the LORD relented from
the disaster that he had spoken of bringing on his people.
(Exod. 32:1–14)

What Moses Knows

I want to show from this text *what Moses knows* and *how Moses
prays* in order to help us to see how *what we know* about God
should affect *how we pray* to God in our lives, in our families, and
in our churches. So we'll start with what Moses knows, and there
are four truths to observe.

1. The perfections of God are unchanging.

When I use the word *perfections* here, I am referring to the
perfect attributes of God that permeate his entire being. These
things never change. God is perfectly holy: "Holy, holy, holy is
the LORD of hosts" (Isa. 6:3). He is without error, he is without
equal, and that will never change. God is perfectly loving: "God is
love . . ." (1 John 4:16). God not only demonstrates love; he defines
it. God is perfectly just: "A God of faithfulness and without iniquity, just and upright is he" (Deut. 32:4).

Just ponder the paradoxical perfections of God. He is perfectly transcendent and perfectly immanent at the same time.
He is perfectly holy and perfectly loving at the same time. He is
perfectly self-existent and perfectly self-sufficient. He is perfectly

omniscient, omnipotent, and omnipresent, all at the same time, and in *all* of these attributes he says in Malachi 3:6, "I the Lord do not change." He does not "change like shifting shadows" (James 1:17 NIV). He is the same "yesterday and today and forever" (Heb. 13:8). Psalm 90:2 is true: "from everlasting to everlasting, [God] is God." The perfections of God are unchanging, and Moses knew this.

Moses begins his prayer in Exodus 32:11 with "O LORD." He calls on the covenant name of God, the Name that represents God's revelation of himself in Exodus 3. Moses goes on to acknowledge God's wrath while appealing to God's love; he acknowledges God's might while appealing to God's mercy; he acknowledges God's glory while pleading for God's goodness. Moses' prayer is plainly grounded in the unchanging perfections of God.

Like Moses, we know that God does not change, and we know this is a good thing. For if God could change, that would mean he could change for the better or for the worse, neither of which would be good. If God could change for the worse, we would have no foundation for our faith and a faint hope on which to hold. Similarly, if God could change for the better, then that would mean he wasn't the best possible Being in the first place. How could we be sure, then, that he's the best possible Being now? Mark it down: God is not malleable. He is not open or progressive, gradually learning or subtly growing. Matthew 5:48 says that our "heavenly Father is perfect"—period.

2. The purposes of God are unchanging.

Moses appeals to the purpose of God in Exodus 32:11–13, saying in essence, "You brought your people out of Egypt for your praise among the Egyptians. Your purpose was not to kill them, but to save them, for your name's sake among the nations. And that purpose," Moses pleads, "has not changed."

Moses is reflecting truth in this prayer that reverberates throughout God's Word. Psalm 33:11 says, "The counsel of the LORD stands forever, the plans of his heart to all generations." Similarly, Isaiah 46:10–11 says, "My counsel shall stand, and I will accomplish all my purpose. . . . I have spoken, and I will bring it to pass; I have purposed, and I will do it." Moses knows that the aims of God do not undergo amendment or adjustment, because the aims of God are always achieved. Moses knows, and we must never forget, that God governs every detail on the globe for the glory of his name. His purposes are unchanging.

3. The promises of God are unchanging.

What shockingly bold language in Exodus 32:13! Moses says "Remember" to God. Remember? To the omniscient God who not only knows all things, but also ordains all things and knows all things that he has ordained at all times. Moses has the appalling audacity to say to God, "Maybe you need to remember something." Remember Abraham? Remember Isaac? Remember Israel? Moses points to the patriarchs and he says, "You promised them that you would give their family the land to which you are now leading them. You cannot go back on your word."

Moses knows Numbers 23:19, that "God is not a man, that he should lie, or a son of man, that he should change his mind. Has he said, and will he not do it? Or has he spoken, and will he not fulfill it?" Moses knows what the psalmist will later say in Psalm 33:4: "For the word of the LORD is upright, and all his work is done in faithfulness." He knows what God himself will say in Psalm 89: "I will not violate my covenant or alter the word that went forth from my lips" (v. 34). Praise God for this reality. Praise God that his promises are not pathetic. Praise God that his promise of forgiveness is not feeble. Praise God that his promise of unending life *with* him is not in doubt because of unforeseen limits *in* him.

Jesus says, "Heaven and earth will pass away, but my words will not pass away" (Matt. 24:35). Moses knows that the promises of God are unchanging. Isn't it interesting that in the very passage in the Old Testament that sparks the most discussion today about what changes in God, Moses bases his entire prayer on that which never changes in God?

That brings us to Exodus 32:14, where the Bible tells us that "the LORD relented from the disaster that he had spoken of bringing on his people." So how are we to understand this? Amidst all that is unchanging in God, it certainly seems like something changed here. Just four verses before this, God said to Moses, "Now therefore let me alone, that my wrath may burn hot against them and I may consume them, in order that I may make a great nation of you" (v. 10). Now God relents. The word *relented* is translated in some Bibles as "repented," and in others, "He changed his mind." It's the same word that's used in other places in Scripture to describe how *people* change their mind. It's also the same word that's used in some places in Scripture (like Num. 23:19) to describe how God *doesn't* change his mind. Likewise, 1 Samuel 15:29 says, "He who is the Glory of Israel does not lie or change his mind; for he is not a human being, that he should change his mind" (NIV). So what is going on here? This is where the next truth of this text comes to the fore.

4. The plan of God is unfolding.

God is perfectly sovereign. His purposes are fixed. He is faithful to his promises. He does all that he pleases. This is obviously important, for if God's plan is not fixed, then God's plan is apparently out of his control. This is what a variety of popular and practical theologies would claim today. They say that God is not sure what is going to happen next in history. He is responding to the wants and whims of man. And ultimately, they say, God doesn't know what he's doing. This is heresy.

God *does* know what he's doing, and God *is* ordaining all that is happening. When we come to Exodus 32, we must realize that God is not surprised by what's taking place here. God is not surprised when his people sin, *and* God is not surprised when Moses prays. God's will is as settled in Exodus 32 as it is anywhere else in Scripture. But we have this story for a reason—for it shows us the unfolding plan of God.

This story powerfully portrays how God judges men in their sin. The people of Israel sin grievously against God. That's why God says, "They have turned away. They are stiff-necked. And they are worthy of destruction . . . of death." That's true. Remember, this is the unchanging character of God. He is holy, and he will judge men in their sin. Sin is an infinite offense in his sight, and sin demands his swift, white-hot wrath. So in verses 9–10, we see that God judges men in their sin.

But then God provides a mediator for sinners.

This is the whole picture that Exodus has given us to this point. Moses is the covenant mediator, the one who goes back and forth between God and his people, the one who stands before the people on God's behalf and stands before God on the people's behalf. God had set it up that way. So when you get to Exodus 32:7, God says to Moses, "Go down . . ." Consider this: If God was going to destroy the Israelites on the spot, then why would he send Moses down? The answer is that God was planning to spare his people through Moses' mediation.

The reality of Exodus 32 is crystal clear: God will demonstrate his wrath against the people of Israel *unless* a man steps in and mediates on their behalf. All this squares with the unchanging perfections of God. God is holy and just; he will punish sin. At the same time, he is loving and merciful, and he will be true to his covenantal promise to save this contemptible people. How does he do it? How is God true to his unchanging perfections and his unchanging promises while fulfilling his unchanging purposes? He does it through an unfolding plan. He appoints a mediator to stand in the gap for sinners.

Isn't it ironic that at the beginning of this chapter, the people virtually disown the only one who can stand before God on their behalf (Exod. 32:1)? Yet in the middle of the chapter, we see Moses doing exactly that, interceding for them. And in so doing, Moses is not changing the plan that God had offered. He is fulfilling the plan that God had ordained.

A Familiar and Gracious Plan

This unfolding plan of God is not unfamiliar to us in Scripture. We think of Jonah, whom God sent to Nineveh to proclaim this word: "Yet forty days, and Nineveh shall be overthrown!" (Jonah 3:4). Nineveh was going to be destroyed because of their sin in forty days—that's what God *said*. At the same time, though, God *sent* his prophet to tell them that. Why would God do that? It's the same picture we're seeing in Exodus 32. God was judging the Ninevites in their sin. Yet he sent a preacher to warn them. So Jonah, after spending a few days in the digestive system of a fish, does in fact warn them, and this is what happened in Jonah 3:10: "When God saw what they did, how they turned from their evil way, God relented of the disaster that he had said he would do to them, and he did not do it." God judges sin *and* he provides a mediator through whom he displays his mercy.

But we don't look ultimately to Jonah in order to understand this unfolding plan of God. Brothers and sisters, we look to Jesus. This is the gospel. In our sin, you and I stand under the judgment of a holy God, and he is compelled by the perfection of his character to condemn us. Death is not a hypothetical possibility for us; it is our sure and certain penalty, a concrete reality for you and me in our sin. But, praise be to God, he has provided a mediator! It is ironic, isn't it? The very One we despise is the only One who can stand before God on our behalf. And God says to him, "Go down, Jesus. Go down because your people have become corrupt. They have turned away from me in idolatry and immorality, and unless you intercede for them, they will surely be destroyed by my wrath." And Jesus comes down, he stands in the gap as a substitute for sinners, and—because of his sacrifice—God relents his wrath from you and me.

I am eternally grateful for the unfolding plan of God—that this God, unchanging in his perfect justice and grace, purposed from eternity past to save me from my sin for his name's sake. He promised to raise me up to new life with him, and he did it all through the mediation of his Son on my behalf. God's perfections, God's purposes, and God's promises are unchanging, yet his plan is ever unfolding—under his providence, mind you—and in his perfect plan, it makes perfect sense for God in his mercy to say, "Man's sin warrants my wrath, yet I will raise up a man to mediate on their behalf, and I will relent."

Providence and Prayer

In all of this, see how it is that what Moses knows determines the way Moses prays. See how Moses' doctrine of providence drives him to prayer. He knows God is in control of all things, and he knows that doesn't make prayer meaningless. Instead, Moses knows that God has ordained prayer as a means by which he can (and must) participate in God's plan. He knows God has purposes, and he believes God is going to use his prayers to accomplish those purposes.

Do we realize what's going on here? God, in his providence, has chosen to make prayer a powerful means by which we interact with him and effectively shape the course of history. That is not an overstatement: this statement booms across the pages of the Bible. People pray, and fire falls from heaven. People pray, and the lame walk, the hungry eat, and the dead come to life.

Look at the story of the church in Acts: every major move of God in that book comes about in response to the prayers of God's people. They're gathered together in chapter 1, devoted to *prayer*, and in chapter 2 the Spirit of God pours out on them like flames of fire, and three thousand people are saved. In chapter 3, Peter and John go up to the temple at the time of *prayer*, and by the beginning of chapter 4, "Many of those who had heard the word believed, and the number of the men came to about five thousand" (4:4). In chapter 6, they devote themselves to the ministry of *prayer* and the Word, and immediately we learn that "the number of the disciples multiplied greatly in Jerusalem" (6:7). At the end of chapter 7, Stephen looks up to heaven and *prays*, and right after that in chapter 8, the church scatters to Judea and Samaria preaching the gospel wherever they go. In chapter 9 Paul is saved and he connects with Ananias, all in the context of *prayer*. We see the same thing in chapter 10, as Peter and Cornelius are *praying*, and the door is opened for the spread of the gospel to the nations. When we get to chapter 12, Peter's in jail and the church is *praying*, and an angel pokes him on the side and then leads him outside. In chapter 13 church leaders are worshiping and *fasting* and *praying*, and the Spirit says, "Set apart for me Barnabas and Saul for the work to which I have called them" (13:2). Out of this, a missionary movement begins that turns the Roman Empire upside down. Finally, in chapter 16 Paul and Silas are *praying* in the middle of prison. God responds with an earthquake, and a jailer and his family are saved.

I say it again: God, in his providence, has not called us in prayer to *watch* history, but to *shape* history for the glory of his great name. Now I know that some (maybe many!) are still uncomfortable with that kind of language, but let's be clear what we're *not* saying. We're not saying God is an impotent King who's just sitting on his throne waiting for someone to pray so that he can start working in the world. That is not what I'm saying, because that's not what we see in this text. Instead, what we see is a God who wills to work through willing intercessors. What I'm saying is that when we pray, God responds. When we pray, we take our God-given place and use our God-ordained privilege to participate with him in the accomplishment of his purposes on the planet. May God help us to see that Moses prayed, and it had an effect. So with us: we pray, and it will have an effect.

How Moses Prays

So how does Moses' doctrine of providence lead him to pray? And how must *our* doctrine of providence lead *us* to pray? Consider three different ways based on Moses' intercession for the people of Israel.

1. He pleads for God's mercy upon sinners.

"God, save them. God, don't destroy them." Notice the basis for Moses' prayer. He doesn't say to God, "They don't deserve your wrath." No, Moses sees the severity of their sin, and he knows God's wrath is exactly what they deserve. So instead of appealing to some inherent goodness in man, he appeals to the intrinsic glory of God. "Save them, O God, for your Name's sake. Show your majesty by showering them with mercy." And then, later on in the chapter, Moses' intercession intensifies.

So Moses returned to the LORD and said, "Alas, this people has sinned a great sin. They have made for themselves gods of gold. But now, if you will forgive their sin—but if not, please blot me out of your book that you have written." (Exod. 32:31–32)

What a prayer! To pray—just like we will see Paul pray in Romans 9—that he, Moses, would be accursed and cut off for the sake of this people. Now both Moses and Paul know, based upon the purposes and promises of God, that this is not possible, but this is what we mean when we think about *the role of desperate prayer in the mystery of divine providence.* There's a desperation here, an exasperation that says, "God, whatever it takes . . . do whatever it takes . . . take my own life, if necessary . . . but glorify yourself in the salvation of these souls." Is this the way we pray? God, help us to plead like this for the salvation of souls around us here in North America and across the nations.

I recently returned from a trip to Nepal, where a few of our church's pastors and I took off from Kathmandu in a helicopter. We came in at about twelve thousand feet, where we landed in the middle of these mountains at the border of Nepal and Tibet—basically as far as you can go up in these mountains and still maintain life. Then we hiked out about ninety miles over the next six days, going through village after village after village that gave definition to urgent physical and spiritual need. A study was done about ten years ago in these villages in the Himalayas, finding that half the children were dying before their eighth birthday. One mom had fourteen kids: two made it to adulthood. They're dying of things like diarrhea. In one village an outbreak of cholera, an infection of the small intestine that causes diarrhea, led to the deaths of sixty people. There is poverty everywhere.

One of the worst by-products of this poverty is sex trafficking. Traffickers will prey on the people in these villages. The trafficker goes into a village, meets with a family, promises their daughter a better life if she will go with him to the city, and maybe even gives the family money. About one hundred dollars is all it takes to convince a starving family that it's worth selling their daughter off. Besides, she's going to be better off, right? So they give her away, and the traffickers pick up little girls who are ten or fifteen years old—and maybe even younger, at times. They take them to Kathmandu where they put these little girls in a brothel, and they break them. They drug and rape them repeatedly. Then they require them to do whatever the men who come into these brothels want them to do. Some of these little girls will have fifteen customers a day. And this is their life: shamed, used, and abused, and they can't get out. The police are corrupt because they're paid off by the traffickers, and the traffickers threaten to kill the families of the girls if they leave. Some of the girls they keep in Kathmandu; others are taken into India, or the Middle East, or down into North Africa. We're talking thousands and thousands of girls taken from impoverished villages like the ones we were in.

As if that's not enough, on top of the poverty and the sex trafficking, these villages are totally unreached. There are twenty-four Tibetan Buddhist people groups in these villages who are totally unreached with the gospel, which means they've never even heard it. We walked for days without ever meeting someone who had heard of Jesus until we got there. At one point, we were standing on the site of a Hindu holy river, where, according to their tradition, dead bodies are to be brought by family members. Within twenty-four hours of death, they put the dead body on a funeral pyre over the river, and they burn it, letting the ashes go down into the river. This is believed to be helpful in reincarnation. When we turned the corner and saw these funeral pyres spread out across the river, and these families wailing over these bodies, we just stopped. There I stood, looking at physical bodies that were alive the day before, and now I'm watching them burn. I know that what I'm seeing is an earthly representation of a much, much deeper, graver, eternal reality. And as I look at these bodies burning, I realize that most of them never even heard the gospel.

So I'm praying, "God, have mercy on them. God, have mercy on these men and women and their families . . . and these kids . . . and these girls in these brothels." And I'm praying that God, in his providence, might use my pleading, and the pleading of many others, to achieve his purposes in that place, to glorify his name as the Defender of the poor and the Deliverer of the slave and the Savior of the peoples. Jesus has purchased men and women from every single one of those Tibetan Buddhist people groups, so I'm pleading, "God, do whatever it takes . . . use my life however *you* want, to get the praise *you're* due from them!"

2. He pleads for God's presence and power among his people.

Here's what happens in Exodus 33:1–3:

> The LORD said to Moses, "Depart; go up from here, you
> and the people whom you have brought up out of the
> land of Egypt, to the land of which I swore to Abraham,
> Isaac, and Jacob, saying, 'To your offspring I will give it.'
> I will send an angel before you, and I will drive out the
> Canaanites, the Amorites, the Hittites, the Perizzites,
> the Hivites, and the Jebusites. Go up to a land flowing
> with milk and honey; but I will not go up among you,
> lest I consume you on the way, for you are a stiff-necked
> people."

God essentially says to Moses in Exodus 33, "Okay, the land is yours, but I won't go with you." In other words, "You can have my promises, but you can't have my presence." What would you do here if you were in Moses' shoes? Be careful not to answer too quickly, because you and I are tempted in a strangely similar way all across our church culture today. You and I are tempted every day in our lives and in our churches to do the work of God apart from the power of the presence of God. We have created a whole host of means and methods for doing ministry today that require little if any help at all from the Holy Spirit of God. We don't have to fast and pray for the church to grow; we have marketing for that. We can draw the crowds without prayer; we have publicity.

It's dangerously possible for you and me to carry on the machinery and activity of the churches we lead, and all of it can be smooth, even successful; and we may never notice that the Spirit is totally absent from it. If we're not careful, we can deceive ourselves, mistaking the presence of physical bodies in a building for the existence of spiritual life in a church. I wonder if the greatest hindrance to the advancement of the gospel in our day may be the attempt of the people of God to do the work of God apart from the power of the Spirit of God. The greatest barrier to the spread of the gospel may not be the self-indulgent immorality of our culture, but our self-sufficient mentality in the church, which is evident in our prayerlessness.

So, what does Moses do when faced with the prospect of doing God's work apart from God's presence? He prays. He goes into the tent of meeting (Exod. 33:7–11) and he prays:

> Moses said to the LORD, "See, you say to me, 'Bring up this people,' but you have not let me know whom you will send with me. Yet you have said, 'I know you by name, and you have also found favor in my sight.' Now

therefore, if I have found favor in your sight, please show me now your ways, that I may know you in order to find favor in your sight. Consider too that this nation is your people." (Exod. 33:12–13)

Moses knows that there is an obvious discrepancy between what God is calling him to do and the resources he has to do it. He knows he can't do it alone. He needs God to go with him, and he will settle for nothing less. So he stays in the tent until God says, "My presence will go with you, and I will give you rest" (33:14). But even that's not enough for Moses, for he continues, "If your presence will not go with me, do not bring us up from here. For how shall it be known that I have found favor in your sight, I *and* your people? Is it not in your going with *us*, so that *we* are distinct, I *and* your people, from every other people on the face of the earth?" (33:15–16, emphasis added)

Moses doesn't just want God's presence and power with *him*; he wants God's presence and power with *them*—with him *and* the people. He knows there is a corporate element to God's purpose in the world, so he pleads for God's presence and power among his people. We must pray in the same way. We need God to show the power of his presence in the midst of his people in our day.

There is an obvious discrepancy between what God has called us to do and the resources we have in and of ourselves to do it. We cannot shepherd the church in our own skill. We cannot program ministry in the church through our own power. We cannot make disciples in our neighborhoods, and we cannot make disciples among all the nations by mustering up more of our own might. We need God.

We need to fall on our faces and plead for God to show his power in his people. Isn't this why, when you get to the pages of the New Testament, you see so few exhortations to even pray for the lost, yet so many exhortations to pray for God's power in the church? For when God's power is present among his people, the gospel spreads to the lost! In Matthew 9:37–38 Jesus says, "The harvest is plentiful, but the laborers are few; therefore pray earnestly to the Lord of the harvest to send out laborers into his harvest."

The harvest is plentiful! They're waiting to hear! So what do we pray for? We pray, "Lord, wake your people up to go to work! Send people out with power!" This is mind-boggling, that you and I would be called upon by Christ to tell God what he needs to do and who he needs to send in order to accomplish his mission. The mystery of prayer!

Consider Acts 4, when the church was being persecuted. What did they pray? They started with the doctrine of providence:

> "Sovereign Lord, who made the heaven and the earth and the sea and everything in them. . . . Herod and Pontius Pilate [were gathered], along with the Gentiles and the peoples of Israel, to do whatever your hand and your plan had predestined to take place." (vv. 24, 27–28)

They knew their persecution was preordained, so they prayed,

> "And now, Lord, look upon their threats and grant to your servants to continue to speak your word with all boldness, while you stretch out your hand to heal, and signs and wonders are performed through the name of your holy servant Jesus." (vv. 29–30)

And what happened?

> And when they had prayed, the place in which they were gathered together was shaken, and they were all filled with the Holy Spirit and continued to speak the word of God with boldness. (v. 31)

They pleaded for the presence and power of God upon his people, and he answered.

> And with great power the apostles were giving their testimony to the resurrection of the Lord Jesus, and great grace was upon them all. . . . And more than ever believers were added to the Lord, multitudes of both men and women. (4:33; 5:14)

This is what we pray for, and this is how God acts. We pray for the power of God upon the people of God, and God gives it. And the effects give him glory.

So let us not settle for prayerlessness, and in so doing settle for powerlessness. Let us throw aside our damning dependence on natural ability and human ingenuity, and let us plead for *God* to do in our churches, across our country, and among the nations what only *God* can do. In the midst of the Great Awakening, Jonathan Edwards knew that only God is able to do the work of God, and he notes, "When God has something very great to accomplish for his church, it is his will that there should precede it the extraordinary prayers of his people."[37]

3. He pleads for God's glory on the earth.

It's as if Moses has not been bold enough already. God has relented from his wrath, and he has promised his presence among his people. If I'm Moses, I'm content at this point. But not Moses. He has prevailed with God in prayer, yet he tarries in the tent and asks for one more thing. Moses said, "Please show me your glory" (Exod. 33:18).

Just think about the man who is making this request. This is the man who was privileged to speak with God in a bush that blazed with fire but never burned out. This is the man who saw God split a sea in half right before his eyes. This is the man who saw God lead him and his people with a pillar of cloud by day and a pillar of fire by night. This is the man who struck a rock and saw water come pouring out of it to replenish the people. This is the man who prayed for food and saw God send bread from heaven. This is the man who, when everybody else was warned to stay away, was invited to stand on Mount Sinai and commune with God.

If anyone had seen the glory of God, it was Moses. He had seen so much. But here's the deal: he wanted more.

And so Moses prayed, he pleaded, for God to show him the fullness of his glory. God says, "Moses, you don't know what you're asking for." A complete revelation of God in all his glory would annihilate Moses on the spot. Moses is pleading for that which would obliterate him. Yet God agrees to show him his back, a partial view, so to speak, which, according to the next chapter, is a breathtaking glimpse of God's faithfulness and forgiveness, goodness and glory. And *this* is the end of prayer, isn't it? This is the termination of all supplication.

We pray because we want to see God. We pray because we want to know God. Do *you* want to see and know God like that? A. W. Tozer said,

> I want deliberately to encourage this mighty longing after God. The lack of it has brought us to our present low estate. The stiff and wooden quality about our religious lives is a result of our lack of holy desire. Complacency is a deadly foe of all spiritual growth. Acute desire must be present or there will be no manifestation of Christ to his people. He waits to be wanted. Too bad that with many of us He waits so long, so very long, in vain.[38]

We pray because we want God. We want to see him, we want to know him, and we want to glorify him. This is how Jesus taught us to pray: "Our Father in heaven, hallowed be your name. Your kingdom come, your will be done, on earth as it is in heaven" (Matt. 6:9–10). Do you see it? Providence and prayer. His name will be hallowed. His kingdom will come. His will shall be done on earth as it is in heaven. And *all* of these things will happen in response to the prayers of his people.

Revelation 8 tells us that the prayers of the saints are being stored in the heavenly places. They're accumulating at the altar of God. Every single prayer for the kingdom of God to come, and every single prayer for the glory of God to be made known—not one of them is lost in transmission. Not one of them is ever uttered in vain. Every single one of them is fueling the fire of incense that one day—one day soon!—will usher in the climax of all history in the consummation of God's kingdom. So don't underestimate the role of desperate prayer in your life, in your family, in your church, or in the mystery of divine providence in the universe.

Plead for God's mercy upon sinners, for him to relent from his wrath! Plead for God's presence and power among his people, and plead for God's glory on the earth. Plead, and plead some more, and keep on pleading until the day when Scripture promises that we shall see him—"They will see his face" (Rev. 22:4)—in all his unchanging perfections, as all his unchanging purposes and promises come to pass in his ever-unfolding plan of which you and I have the privilege of playing a part.

NOTES

1. John Piper, "The New Calvinism and the New Community," the Gaffin Lecture at Westminster Seminary, March 12, 2014.

2. Iain H. Murray, *Archibald G. Brown: Spurgeon's Successor* (Edinburgh: Banner of Truth, 2011), 367.

3. Jonathan Leeman, ed., *The Underestimated Gospel: Addresses at the 2012 Together for the Gospel Conference* (Nashville, TN: B&H, 2014), 4.

4. "An intemperate, imprudent zeal, and a degree of enthusiasm, soon crept in and mingled itself with that revival of religion" in Jonathan Edwards, *Works, vol. 2* (Edinburgh: Banner of Truth, 2005), 321. See chapter 12 in Iain H. Murray, *Jonathan Edwards: A New Biography* (Edinburgh: Banner of Truth, 1987).

5. For more information, visit Crossway.org. As well as the addresses from 2012, I also quote below from those of 2010, entitled *The (Unadjusted) Gospel* (Wheaton, IL: Crossway, 2014).

6. John Piper, *A Hunger for God: Desiring God through Fasting and Prayer* (Wheaton, IL: Crossway, 1997), 99–100.

7. This foreword has been condensed and adapted from an article in *The Banner of Truth* magazine, No. 609 (June 2014), accessible at http://wbcs.edu/wp/wp-content/uploads/2014/11/609-Jun-2014.pdf.

8. Mark Dever, "How to Survive a Cultural Crisis" (May 13, 2013), http://www.thegospelcoalition.org/article/how-to-survive-a-cultural-crisis.

9. Carl E. Braaten, Robert W. Jenson, eds., *A Map of Twentieth-Century Theology: Readings from Karl Barth to Radical Pluralism* (Minneapolis, MN: Fortress, 1995), 244–45.

10. Brian D. McLaren, *A Generous Orthodoxy* (Grand Rapids, MI: Zondervan/Youth Specialties, 2004), 260.

11. Scripture passages in this chapter are taken from the New American Standard Bible.

12. Walter J. Chantry, *Today's Gospel: Authentic or Synthetic?* (Carlisle, PA: Banner of Truth, 1970), 45–46.

13. Ibid., 48.

14. Terry Johnson, *The Parables of Jesus: Entering, Growing, Living and Finishing in God's Kingdom* (Scotland: Christian Focus, 2007), 286.

15. Charles H. Spurgeon, Sermon #1000, or "Bread Enough and to Spare" in *Miracles and Parables of Our Lord, Vol. 3* (Grand Rapids, MI: Baker, reprinted 2003), 340.

16. Leon Morris, *Luke* (Grand Rapids, MI: Eerdmans, 1974), 267.

17. Ibid.

18. Ibid.

19. Scripture passages in this chapter are taken from the New International Version, 1984 edition.

20. John Wesley, recorded in his journal entry for Tuesday, December 23, 1755, cited in David Poling, ed., *Inspiration Three* (New Canaan, CT: Keats Publishing, Inc., 1973), 119.

21. The themes in this chapter, as well as the specific verses discussed, are explored in greater detail in Kevin DeYoung, *Taking God at His Word: Why the Bible Is Knowable, Necessary, and Enough, and What that Means for You and Me* (Wheaton, IL: Crossway, 2014), see especially pages 95–110. At times, particular sentences, or even a few full paragraphs, are borrowed from this earlier work. Used by permission.

22. Robert Watts, *The Rule of Faith and the Doctrine of Inspiration: The Carey Lectures for 1884* (London: Hodder and Stoughton, 1885), 139.

23. Donald Macleod, "Jesus and Scripture," in *The Trustworthiness of God: Perspectives on the Nature of Scripture,* eds. Paul Helm and Carl Trueman (Grand Rapids, MI: Eerdmans, 2002), 73.

24. Quoted in John Wenham, *Christ and the Bible,* 3rd ed. (Eugene, OR: Wipf and Stock, 2009), 20.

25. Many of these points are drawn from Macleod, "Jesus and Scripture," 91, 95.

26. J. I. Packer, *Truth and Power: The Place of Scripture in the Christian Life* (Wheaton, IL: Harold Shaw, 1996), 55.

27. J. I. Packer, *"Fundamentalism" and the Word of God* (Grand Rapids, MI: Eerdmans, 1958), 61.

28. Ibid., 61–62.

29. Hughes Oliphant Old, *The Reading and Preaching of the Scriptures in the Worship of the Christian Church*, Seven Volumes (Grand Rapids, MI: Eerdmans, 1998–2010).

30. Old, *Reading and Preaching of the Scriptures*, 6:546.

31. Ibid., 573.

32. Ibid., 574.

33. Old, *Reading and Preaching of the Scriptures*, 7:555.

34. Ibid., 556.

35. Ibid., 557–58.

36. D. A. Carson, *A Call to Spiritual Reformation: Priorities from Paul and His Prayers* (Grand Rapids, MI: Baker, Academic, 1992), 9.

37. Jonathan Edwards, *Thoughts on the Revival*, in vol. 1 of *The Works of Jonathan Edwards* (Peabody, MA: Hendrickson Publishers, 2004), 426.

38. A. W. Tozer, *The Pursuit of God* (Camp Hill, PA: Wing Spread Publishers, 1993), 17.

Scripture Index

Acts